china & glass

china & glass

caroline clifton-mogg

photography by **simon upton**

jacqui
small

'For Billy'

First published in 2004 by
Jacqui Small
an imprint of Aurum Press Limited
25 Bedford Avenue
London WC1B 3AT

Publisher: Jacqui Small
Design: Penny Stock
Editors: Kate John, Polly Boyd
Location researcher: Nadine Bazar
Production: Geoff Barlow

ISBN 1-903221-27-7

A catalogue record for this book is
available from the British Library

Printed in China

2006 2005 2004

10 9 8 7 6 5 4 3 2 1

contents

introduction

The search for beautiful and interesting china and glass, whether old or new, perfect or less so, can easily become a pastime and a passion that is both all-absorbing and extremely fulfilling.

Every weekend I make my way on Saturday morning to my nearest antique market which, fortuitously, happens to be Portobello Market in London. Once there, I tack down the road, ducking and diving into the many arcades, each of which holds stall after stall selling everything you could imagine, from scientific instruments and leather hat boxes to fishing reels and costume jewellery. Although often sorely tempted, I generally manage to resist these transient temptations, because it is towards the stalls that sell china and glass that I am consistently and unerringly drawn. Whether very old or fairly new, one-off pieces or mass-produced designs, rustic earthenware, smooth creamware or subtle oriental glazes – all catch my eye and stop me in my tracks.

I am not a purist collector, my specialist knowledge of great porcelain painters or glass blowers is practically non-existent, and in fact I am hardly a collector at all, if that means searching out early Chelsea porcelain, pre-war Whitefriars glass or contemporary studio pieces. For me, perfection is not the first consideration, for what I want are pieces that have immediate visual appeal, even if they are cracked or otherwise imperfect. I do not

Right
This is a perfect example of functional, everyday objects turned into a display: every object on this mantelpiece is not only decorative but is used on a regular basis in the kitchen.

Opposite
A large collection of brown and white ceramics is an integral part of the decorative scheme of this living room. Here, china is used as an alternative to pictures or books, both on the display shelves and on the walls themselves.

necessarily use such objects for the purpose for which they were intended, but that is hardly a new idea – in the 16th century, for example, vessels such as jugs and wine ewers were often used as impromptu vases.

For the china enthusiast there is simply so much scope, with such a huge variety of design and shape available. You might be interested in transfer prints for example, or hand-painted designs. It might be the glaze that catches your eye or the actual shape of the vessel. You might be looking for floral designs – plenty of scope there – or pieces that are ornamented with exotic gilded decoration. There are dishes designed for specific foods such as oysters or asparagus and shaped accordingly, and solitary survivors of once large and ornate services, such as a single perfect cup or plate, as well as part sets – four or six pretty plates of one design that you could use with others of an equally pretty but different pattern.

Glassware can also appeal to collectors of all descriptions: designs may be deeply etched, engraved, moulded, pressed or strictly simple. There are glass jugs, bowls, dishes, plates and, of course, a multitude of designs of drinking glass – these may be tiny or huge, all stem surmounted by a delicate bowl or all bowl with next to no stem. And the shapes – circular, of course, but also conical, square and even twisted.

The search does not, of course, have to be limited to the antique. Modern crockery and contemporary glassware have never been so diverse, and pieces of all kinds are found in every sort of outlet. The large department stores offer an enormous range, while small specialist shops sell limited numbers of carefully chosen individual designs, as do the ever-increasing

specialized mail order companies that often purvey a particular look or theme. Heavy stoneware storage jars are presently on my shopping list, as are new, multi-coloured glass plates, which I want to use mixed together in a kaleidoscope of colour on the table, combined with the few old pieces of coloured glass that I already have.

All china and glass – particularly the sort we use every day – are by definition very much part of our familiar lives. From childhood we are surrounded by dishes and plates, cups and glasses – some old and some new, and many of them well-loved and cherished objects; so it is not surprising that when it comes to setting up our own homes, the china and glass that we choose is as important to us as the furniture or floor coverings. Many people, for example, inherit pieces – perhaps an entire dinner service or set of glasses, or a single beautiful bowl or decanter – and one of the great pleasures in looking for pieces to go into a new home is deciding on how to combine the old with the new, the elaborate with the simple – what to add, what to look for, and whether to mix or match. New china and glass can be combined and grouped with others of its ilk, or mixed with older pieces, using colour, design, shape or pattern as an underlying common theme. As always in decorating, the trick is to balance the look – to combine the old and new in an inventive way that is also practical and pleasing.

You will judge from this that *China & Glass* is not about collecting the grand bravura pieces designed to display and impress; it is instead about all those everyday pieces – both new and old, beautiful and less so, but that we could not live without. Throughout the book we look at how such pieces can be best used at home, whether arranged in a formal group on a mantelpiece, or simply brought out at mealtimes to be noticed and admired. Some solutions involve thought and even pre-thought, others simply consist in letting well alone; it is for us to suggest avenues and ideas that you might care to explore, but ultimately it is for you to consider how you want to use and display your personal collection of china and glass in the way that pleases you most.

Left
Crystal and furnishings designer William Yeoward (see pp.120–21) demonstrates the virtues of the traditional built-in dresser – the ultimate piece of furniture for both display and storage. It takes a very sure eye as well as confidence and taste to arrange so many disparate objects together.

the objects

china shape

The shape of an object was originally determined by practical requirements such as function – for example, whether the item was to serve as a container (and if so, the nature of the contents to be stored), or whether or not it needed to be carried around. Over time, personal taste and increasing interest in decorative display have meant that aesthetics are now as much of a consideration as function, resulting in a wealth of imaginatively shaped, fanciful creations that are endlessly pleasurable to discover.

Previous page
An al fresco display, where decorative white dishes are used to hold fruit, vegetables and flowering plants. By displaying only one type of fruit or vegetable in each dish, the shape of the china is seen to best advantage.

Opposite
A fine piece of antique creamware with its characteristic relief moulding and pierced decoration. Originally, it was used as a dish for strawberries or other soft fruit that needed drainage holes.

plates

Plates have been used for the serving or holding of food ever since the ritual of eating became a social function rather than simply a biological necessity. Medieval meals, often taken in company in feudal halls, were eaten from a trencher – a thick slab of bread, often trimmed into a square or a rectangle, which was used as a base onto which pieces taken from a central dish were placed to be eaten with the fingers. In her absorbing book *The Rituals of Dinner*, Margaret Visser says that today, dishes that involve serving a piece of meat or a bird on a piece of bread are the last survivors of that ancient custom.

By the 14th century, the bread trencher often sat on a wooden or pewter underplate, and by the 16th century the bread had all but disappeared and people used individual serving dishes, made of earthenware, which more closely resembled a bowl than a modern plate. By the end of the 17th century, this dish had become circular and flat and the dinner plate as we know it now was in use – at least in the more sophisticated dining halls of Europe.

The emergence of the dinner plate corresponded with a general acceptance of personal cutlery – or at any rate of the fork, the individual knife having been a fixture since medieval dinners, where each man brought his own knife which was used both to cut and to eat from; a fork needed a hard surface on which to operate effectively, and metal or ceramics were obviously more resistant than wood.

Top left
Service plates often take the place of table mats. Peri Wolfman (see pp.136–37) always uses extra-large buffet plates from US-based china company Williams-Sonoma, on which she places a series of dishes throughout the meal.

Top right
Victoria du Roure (see pp.128–29), for her restaurant Home Hill in New Hampshire, had porcelain dishes especially made by Bernadout of Limoges, in shapes and designs that she felt would complement her subtle, often elegant recipes.

Opposite
The shape of a plate is dictated by fashion as well as function, and both Eastern and Western cooks feel that food, no matter how simple, is enhanced by a beautiful, well-designed plate.

Right
Where plates and other dishes are of varying design, the colour should be one that does not detract from the shapes. Here, all-white dishes keep the place setting simple and attractive.

Above and opposite
The variety of plate shapes now available is legion: New York fashion designer Reem Acra (see pp.134–35) mixes East and West, using hand-decorated plates from the Lebanon, on top of plain pink squared plates from the US manufacturer Lenox, which act as the frame for this highly decorated picture. The combination is both ornate and delicate.

The same sequence of developments had taken place in North America, where early settlers had first used trenchers of wood, and later pewter or earthenware, until the end of the 19th century, when ceramic plates were the norm.

There has always been a vast difference between the presentation of a formal and informal table, and of course informal, day-to-day domestic eating has always been a more relaxed affair, with utensils that are simpler in style, usually made from a sturdier material such as earthenware pottery, decorated and glazed. Formal dinner plates were not only usually of a porcelain type and more finely decorated, they were also different in shape, always having a shallow rim as opposed to the flat plate used for breakfast and luncheon – a difference still seen today in traditional services.

The banquet, as presented in European courts and noble houses, was an opportunity to impress and influence. Until the early 18th century, European grand banquets would have both serving dishes and individual plates made from silver, but by the end of the 18th century these were replaced by fine porcelain, either exported from China or made in Europe; these porcelain dinner plates were usually highly decorated and gilded. At a formal dinner, dessert was a completely separate course from the rest of the meal and was always served on a table that had been completely cleared and re-laid, or even, depending on the grandeur of the host and setting, presented in a completely different venue – another room perhaps, or even another building in the grounds, such as a folly or summerhouse. It follows that the plates for dessert were also quite different in style and pattern from the rest of a formal service, a fashion that is still followed at today's banquets, notably at Buckingham Palace. Often designed as a set, with each plate a different aspect of a theme or design, they were far more elaborate than the other plates and were intended to be admired and discussed as well as eaten from.

For the 19th-century diner, the modish design motto 'less is more' would have appeared risible. For the rich, in particular, more was definitely more, and this extended to the variety of individual plates (and for that matter knives, forks and spoons, too) that they deemed necessary, or at any rate desirable at the table, necessity in this case being not the mother of invention – rather, a fervent imagination.

serving dishes & platters

While medieval man was eating off bread or wood trenchers, the serving dishes themselves were already an important part of a noble's inventory. Every great hall, and later grand dining room, had a display of the owner's silver plate on show, much of it in the shape of chargers and serving dishes – not that much would be served on them, status and wealth being the purpose of the display rather than more practical considerations.

Once the European ceramic industry had come into being in the 18th century, a wealth of inventiveness and imagination on the potters' part went into creating new shapes and designs for serving dishes and plates; by the 19th century, formal serving dishes might include a roast-meat platter with indented channels for gravy, through which the meat juices could run to be spooned over the meat, as well as a draining dish pierced with holes through which the juices of boiled meats or fish could drain. There were covered meat and vegetable dishes, and fish-shaped platters

Opposite and right
Is it the serving dish that dictates the contents or vice versa? Whichever you believe, the shape and design of the dish does set the tone for food. Here, an unadorned oval white dish is used for green apples, drawing attention to the inviting green of the fruit. Simple, modern dishes such as this can always be bought from such nationwide suppliers as the Ikea chain and Habitat in Europe, and Pottery Barn and Crate and Barrel in the US.

Above
New York-based interior designer Anthony Cochrane collects china from whatever source he can find; his interest is in creating an appetising composition, which he achieves here with his delicious chocolate bombe and accompanying berries served on a simple, heavy white square dish that complements the food.

Right

The idea of specific dishes designed for certain foods has been in existence for hundreds of years; popular in the 18th and 19th centuries were asparagus dishes, which were oval or rectangular and often contained a central smaller, lidded dish that held a sauce or melted butter.

Below

Always collectable are the endless variations on the much-loved blue and white patterned china. A large collection of old blue and white serving dishes could offer a great variety of designs without a single repetition of pattern.

designed in the form of their piscine occupants-to-be, namely salmon, turbot or other fish delicacies. There were dishes with their own warming devices, as well as sauce dishes such as the 'Argyll' – a gravy dish with an inner compartment for hot water, which kept the liquid hot. One oddity was pie dishes made from what was known as 'pastry-ware', in which pastry-less pies, tarts and stews could be made; the ware was biscuit-coloured, unglazed stoneware, which did indeed resemble rather undercooked pastry, and which often came complete with raised leaf decoration, crimped edges and fork holes.

Whimsy also found a place in the design of the serving dish: for the heightened enjoyment of seasonal delicacies, there were asparagus dishes (see above), often with painted, relief-moulded asparagus spears, oyster dishes with oyster-shaped depressions, and crab dishes that were shaped,

Opposite

Green majolica ware was particularly popular in the 19th century, and any number of designs for serving dishes were produced, such as this compote dish filled with deep red raspberries. The pleasure of this combination comes from seeing such deep, rich colours complementing each other in such a satisfying manner.

not surprisingly, like a crab. This whimsical vein was seen again during the first half of the 20th century, when Staffordshire potteries produced many novelty designs for the table. Often brightly coloured, many of them were based on the idea of relief moulding or *trompe l'oeil* representing the form of the animal or vegetable to be served, for example lobster dishes with legs that resembled claws, nut bowls shaped like autumn leaves and featuring ceramic moulded nuts, and fruit bowls in the form of apples or melons; many of these can still be found and some, such as those made by Carlton Ware and Shelley, are much sought after by collectors.

For the dessert course – whether light or elaborate – one could also find specially designed serving dishes. There were ceramic *trompe l'oeil* baskets for chestnuts, grapes and oranges, and for juicy fruits such as strawberries there were shallow dishes with drainage holes that came with matching stands.

Left
Left
This relief-moulded bread crock may well be from the famous Bennington works of Vermont, a well-established American pottery known for its distinctive blue and brownish mottled glazes which appear to trickle down the sides of the vessels.

Below
Small bowls are always useful, both for storage and presentation. The beauty of white ceramics is that their neutral tones not only go with everything around them, but they also enhance other textures and materials such as this country loaf on its antique bread board.

There was even a specific dish for the pineapple, an exotic novelty that had been introduced into England in the 17th century; it consisted of a shallow plate on which stood a low, cup-shaped container, the size of an average pineapple base. Another dish, the tazza, was used both as decoration and for serving fruit and sweetmeats; it was a shallow, round dish on a pedestal foot, a design that derived from the classical.

Cheese had long been an important part of a nourishing meal, and the cheese course had its own range of serving dishes: there was the cheese cradle, which resembled the shape of a rocking chair bow and was designed to hold large, heavy farmhouse cheeses, and the Stilton cheese pan, which was a round pottery dish under a pottery cover, the material being a practical way of keeping the cheese moist. More common was a Stilton cheese stand – a flat dish with a low raised edge and a glass cover, few of which survive.

jugs & containers

Since ceramic objects were first used, the jug or pitcher has always been one of the most popular of vessels: indeed, medieval jugs found today are often carefully modelled and decorated – indications of their importance and value. They were used not only as dispensers of liquids, but also as carriers, for in the days before instant packaging, or indeed mass production, the jug was carried to the source to collect the wine, beer, milk or water that was needed.

Larger jugs include utilitarian kitchen pitchers, fat-bellied harvest jugs (used to carry refreshment to thirsty workers in the fields) or decorative ewers (used to carry hot water throughout the house). Milk jugs are traditionally smaller and more delicate, and sometimes highly decorated; they can be found in a wide variety of shapes, and were often modelled on silver jugs of the time. They were often part of a set of three, each size correspondingly larger than the other. A shallower, small jug, more boat shaped, and often with a foot, was designed as a sauce boat or cream jug, sometimes made with a matching stand. Often designed with a great deal of imagination and originality, they were much in demand in both the dining room and drawing room.

Left
The variety of jug shapes – whether they are old or new – is always fascinating, and they look as pretty on their own for display purposes as they do in more practical settings. Here, Irish designer and writer Trish Foley uses a tall pitcher as a container for dried hydrangea heads, the contrast of textures being particularly pleasing.

Although most jugs have been designed primarily for utilitarian purposes, however refined, there have also always been jugs created principally for decorative purposes. Jugs are the perfect vehicles for a potter's flights of fancy – lips were sometimes curved in the shape of a leaf, a bird or an animal's head, and handles in the form of branches and trunks, flowers and leaves, fruit and vegetables, and animals and humans. Consider the generic toby jug, first made in the 18th century by the famous potter Ralph Wood of Staffordshire, and supposedly inspired by a song of 1761 about a well-known inebriate called Toby Philpot or Fillpot, and made in its thousands ever since. Commemorative jugs have also been popular, particularly in the 18th and 19th centuries; some were painted, while others were decorated with relief moulding, featuring contemporary heroes such as Nelson or Wellington, kings and queens, and national events.

From the 17th century, ceramic bottles came into use – for wine, which was decanted into them from large casks, as well as water and beer. The bottles were reused, and many can still be found today.

Top and above
The shape of jugs developed from their practical functions – from wide-necked, generously bowled jugs for easy pouring, to tall, narrow pitchers for keeping liquids cool or hot.

Right
Cream jugs were often very decorative. They could be made of silver or ceramic and were developed from the curved shape of earlier silver sauce boats.

Below
Jugs of varying periods and designs
look great mixed together, especially
when they share a colour or motif.
Here, neutral tones bind a 19th-
century jug with raised moulding
and an earlier, fat-bellied design
with a sweeping, leaf-ended handle.

Opposite
Creamware allowed ceramic makers
to indulge in shape and design in a
highly imaginative way. Here,
shallow sauce boats or creamers
are displayed alongside pieces with
pierced decoration and side dishes
designed to look like shells.

bowls & tureens

Opposite
Elegant and curving like an upturned wedding hat, the shape of this distinctive bowl defines the dish and vice versa, says chef Victoria du Roure (see pp.128–29).

Left
A bowl on a foot is an elegant object – a classical shape that, like a tight-waisted dress, enhances whatever is inside it.

Below
The proportions of a bowl, the relationship of the height to the width, directly affect the aesthetic pleasure the piece gives.

In medieval Europe, semi-liquid soups and stews with sauce were served in bowls that were shared between couples. The most elemental of designs, the bowl has developed into so many different variations – each with a particular use – particularly in the inventive stage of 18th- and 19th-century potteries.

In the kitchen, of course, earthenware bowls and containers were used for many purposes, from storage to food preparation. Many surviving examples from the 18th and 19th centuries are charming in their imaginative design, for example the lidded egg dishes with relief-moulded, painted chickens on their nests that are so popular with collectors. Other pleasing shapes included unglazed butter pots, which sat in glazed dishes filled with cold water, thus keeping the butter cool, and heavy stoneware mortar and pestles used, as they are today, for grinding spices.

In the 18th-century drawing room there were tea bowls, as well as the accompanying slop bowls into which tea leaves were emptied. At the dining table there were finger bowls, which were originally used more robustly than they are today. Until the early 19th century, the napkin was dipped into the finger bowl and then used to vigorously wipe the hands and mouth; in late 19th-century polite French society, the water in finger bowls was used as a mouth-rinse – the water being taken into the mouth, swished around and then spat out into an accompanying deep saucer.

Left
Early potters often sponged and stencilled patterns to decorate basic and functional pottery, and these dishes are good modern examples. They are lustre-glazed, another traditional decorative technique (see p.55).

Below
This design, with its subtle relief moulding and glaze, is a contemporary take on traditional moulded ware, and was chosen by Swedish interior designer Moussie Sayers to be sold in her London shop, Nordic Style.

Later, fingertips only were acceptable in the water, and the finger bowl had become almost ornamental.

Also in the 18th-century dining room were found any number of serving bowls of different shapes and sizes – shallow or deep, large or small. Doubtless due to the relatively large expanse of ceramic body, bowls have always been vehicles for decorative inventiveness, and 18th- and early 19th-century potters seemed to take great pleasure in adorning such vessels. Some were decorated with painting and prints, while others were embellished with moulded relief in the form of leaves, fruit and vegetables, flowers and birds, and garlands and bows.

Larger bowls with lids were produced, called tureens, the lid being essential for keeping the liquids hot after the often-long journey from the kitchen. At the other extreme, there was the ice-cream tureen, which was a deep, lidded bowl, inside which was a base in which crushed ice was put; a liner above held the ice cream. Ice-cream tureens were often ornately

Left
There is no such thing as a useless bowl. These simple and traditional-shaped bowls are by different makers and collected on the basis that from cotton wool to soup, they will all be used somewhere in the house.

Bottom left
The traditional pudding bowl has a long and honourable history. Originally used to cook steamed puddings in, savoury or sweet, it is still indispensable for storage and cooking, mixing and measuring.

Below
Modern versions of classical shapes, these simple bowls – each slightly differing in design and form – are profoundly satisfying to look at and to use.

Left
A pattern based on lavender sprigs is the theme of these covered soup bowls, designed in Moustiers, in southern France.

Bottom left
Extremely simple, yet so elegant, this antique tureen in white-glazed earthenware is both rare and beautiful. The shape of the tureen has changed little in 300 years; they are the paradigm of functional elegance.

Below
This antique hand-painted and gilded porcelain tureen has a lid topped with a delicate raised rose bud, which echoes the painted roses on the sides and on the matching dinner plates.

Opposite
This classic white soup tureen, with its own china ladle, is a contemporary piece but is little changed from its antique counterpart (see below left).

decorated and sometimes starred as dessert centrepieces. Like bowls, tureens have always been vehicles for moulded designs, but many tureen designs give a fair imitation of the complete vegetable or fruit – particularly rounded varieties such as melons or pumpkins (see p.136), where the lid can be incorporated into the form of the vegetable.

In the bedroom, bowls were needed to hold the hot water transported in ewers, and oval-shaped, straight-sided foot-baths – often used today as pot-plant holders – were also a popular necessity. Also in the shape of a bowl – or sometimes a very large cup – were pottery chamber pots. In the 18th- and early 19th-centuries, these were used not only in the bedroom but were often brought after dinner into the drawing room, to be used by the ladies after they had retired from the dining room, and into the dining room itself, where they were used by the gentlemen of the party.

teapots, cups & mugs

Opposite
A 19th-century moulded Parian ware teapot, with the metal hinged lid typical of the period, is set off by very modern white earthenware, the chunky designs of which accentuate the fine moulding of the teapot.

Left
An antique creamware teapot and assorted creamware cups – remnants of an age when the making and taking of tea was an important daily ceremony – are displayed with other contemporary pieces of this delicate china.

Below
Porcelain and bone china tea services have been a staple of the well-dressed tea tray for 250 years, and many of the patterns favoured and bought today from makers such as Wedgwood and Spode were first produced in the 18th and early 19th centuries. In the 17th century, silver had been the preferred material for teapots until it was overtaken by the less expensive china.

The famous tea ceremony in Japan is as much a ritual for admiring the often valuable and rare utensils, many of which are used only at this event, as it is an occasion to taste tea. While in the West we may not lay quite as much store by our tea services as the Japanese, the teapot has a long and illustrious history, particularly of course in Britain.

Tea was introduced from the East in the late 17th century and immediately became the fashionable beverage, together with the equally foreign and exciting coffee and chocolate. It became *de rigeur* for any lady of note to serve tea at least once a day, for which she needed one of the special sets designed for its serving and drinking; these were first ordered from China, and later from the new manufacturers of Europe. Tea was expensive initially, and teapots were correspondingly small, often holding only enough for one connoisseur; as tea became cheaper, pots became larger, although some of the very large ones still to be found were not always designed for tea – many of them were made as punch pots, used to serve the warming evening drink.

Below
Japanese and Chinese tea bowls are available in Asian shops and can be bought to mix and match. Continental drinkers often prefer bowls like these to cups, particularly for coffee.

Bottom left
The pieces of this 'service' were in fact bought separately, with the Bavarian coffee pot and most of the cups and saucers found in various flea markets in New York and London. The small cup holding spoons is actually a candle holder bought in Paris.

Right
This antique blue and white tea cup and saucer, although European in origin, is clearly influenced by 18th-century Chinese export ware.

The fact that teapots have always been vehicles for the wildest flights of fancy have made them eminently collectable. In addition to the original, rounded shape, they can be found in ovals, oblongs, squares and hexagons. More fanciful shapes include cottages, castles, elephants and monkeys – the variety is endless.

Coffee and chocolate pots were also fashionable from the late 17th century. These were originally made of silver, and the first ceramic pots followed the silversmiths' shapes. Taller than teapots, they were often part of a set with coffee cans and cups.

Opposite
This tea set is modern but based on a neoclassical, early 19th-century design.

The first items of Chinese porcelain imported to Europe in the 17th century were tea bowls, for drinking the new, fashionable brew. By the 18th century, the new European manufacturers had produced their own tea bowls. These were originally modelled on the Chinese, but because it could be uncomfortable to hold this small, fragile, rather hot bowl, handles were gradually introduced, transforming the bowl, by the 19th century, into the cup. They were light and delicate because by then potters had developed a compound that was to be known as bone china, which combined Cornish clay and powdered bone and gave a lightweight, delicate body which promised to be both a successful, and cheaper, alternative to oriental porcelain.

The introduction of the cup gave rise to the saucer. This shallow dish – originally designed, as its name implies, for holding sauce – was paired with the new cup, and was sometimes used as a vessel from which to drink the slightly cooled tea. The custom of drinking from the saucer waned in Europe, although in America it lingered on with the use of cup-plates. These were usually made of glass, on which the empty cups were placed while the tea was drunk from the saucer. This tradition finally died out in the 1850s, when saucers became flatter and shallower; the saucer was now held in one hand and the cup in the other. Another unusual saucer was known as the 'trembleuse'; designed for the shaky-handed, it consisted of a slightly tapered cup that sat in a saucer that resembled an upturned hat, with a well in the middle that held the cup.

The institution of afternoon tea became fashionable in England by the middle of the 19th century. The components needed to undertake this ritual could be extensive: they might include a teapot and stand, a sugar box or bowl, a milk ewer, and a slop bowl for the leaves. There would be large plates for bread and butter, and later for small cakes, and sometimes covered dishes for hot muffins and small plates on which to put them.

Coffee cups, or straight-sided coffee cans, had always been taller than the tea bowl/cup and were originally also used without saucers. Other cup shapes popular in the early 19th century included custard and syllabub cups and moustache cups; the latter had a narrow porcelain guard fixed within the rim, which protected the often long, and elaborately waxed, male moustache from drooping and then melting in the hot liquid.

The pottery mug evolved from the pewter tankard in the 1700s. Then, as now, mugs were often designed as commemorative pieces, and examples were found in almost every home championing the triumphs of contemporary heroes, and recording historical and patriotic events.

Opposite
A collection of different makes and designs of modern china, belonging to Peri Wolfman and Charlie Gold (see pp.136–37), all in varying tones of white and cream. Cups and saucers are stacked like acrobats on a ceramic fish drainer, and shells are placed in a shallow cream china trough.

Above
A modern update on the traditional concept of a tea cup is this delicate ceramic beaker with its filigree silver lid, which acts as a strainer or infuser for the tea. Made by Ted Muehling in Bavaria, it is a fine piece of contemporary design.

Right
There is something about a mug – its solid, earthy shape and comfortable connotations have universal appeal, and they are as popular today as they were 300 years ago, when the ceramic mug was first developed from the pewter tankard.

china colour

Colour has been used in the making of ceramics for thousands of years. Excavated finds show that even in Neolithic times people added colour to their otherwise basic pots. However, it is the Chinese who transformed the art of ceramics over 2,000 years ago, developing and defining the most subtle, delicate glazes ever seen; their sophisticated and refined palette – the softest of creams, pinks, cloud-greys and river-greens – still sets the standards by which all others, even today, are judged.

Opposite
This cheery, inviting table setting happily combines antique green majolica placed on a colourful modern tin plate. The design of the modern piece is taken from an antique porcelain plate and is one of a range at the Dining Room Shop in Barnes, London.

white ceramics

In China, a land that for many centuries was both geographically and politically isolated from the rest of the world, the development of ceramics – earthenware, stoneware, and particularly porcelain, which the Chinese discovered as early as the 7th century – was of an infinitely higher standard than the more rough-and-ready pieces produced in Europe during the same period. For example, while potters in 13th-century China were making shallow ceramic bowls carved with delicate scrolled patterns beneath a soft blue glaze, in England medieval earthenware pots were pretty basic in shape and craftsmanship, decorated with lead glazes either stained green with copper oxide or a yellowish brown using iron.

In the world of ceramics, white has always been the Holy Grail of all glazes, to be endlessly strived for. From the early 17th century, when European potters first saw examples of translucent white Chinese porcelain, made from clay containing kaolin and felspar, they worked hard to develop the same pure white tone; in doing so, they discovered many other bodies and finishes, so that in a sense the whole history of colour in ceramics is tied up with, and dependent on, the search for true white.

Opposite
White is always right and at its best, nothing looks better. Simple, pure and fresh, the key to success lies in the shapes, like the bowls of these generously rounded cups.

Below
Scandinavian style has always been pure and simple. This table consists of white china and clear glass tied together with a central runner – a contemporary update of a 19th-century favourite.

In every country of Europe, manufacturers worked to develop a local as-white-as-possible porcelain. It is thought that the Meissen factory in Germany may well have created the first true European porcelain in the early 1700s – certainly it was white, and they worked further to develop it throughout the 18th century to make it even whiter.

Manufacturers in England were slower to develop porcelain, but experimented with refining earthenware, which has a naturally dark body that fires to a variety of colours from buff to brown, and stoneware, which has a naturally grey body that fires to grey or buff. By the 18th century, developments meant that the grey tone of stoneware had been transformed into a whiter finish by many potteries. The stoneware that was first produced in Staffordshire in the 1700s, possibly by Josiah Spode (1754–1827), was fairly light and white, and was decorated with finesse. Thomas Whieldon and then Josiah Wedgwood (1730–95) continued to experiment for a white ceramic body, and from the 1720s introduced their answer – creamware, a fine whitish earthenware, finished with a clear lead glaze (see pp.46–47, 154–55). It was considerably less expensive than Chinese porcelain, and Wedgwood set about developing its full potential.

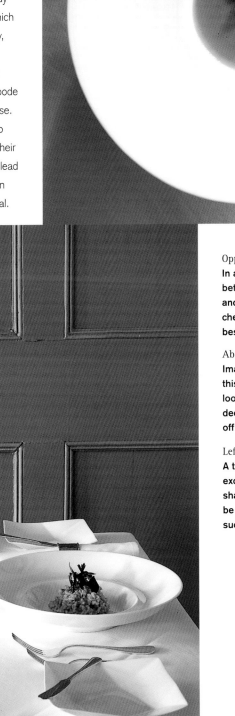

Opposite
In a formal setting, nothing looks better than white. Carefully chosen and displayed, this selection of cheese and fruit is set off at its best on a rectangular white dish.

Above
Imagine how much less interesting this thick green soup would have looked against coloured china; the deep rim of this white bowl sets it off to perfection.

Left
A table without elaboration or excess invariably looks best. The shapes of the white china need to be varied and interesting to make such a pleasing setting.

Opposite
Creamware was 18th-century England's answer to Chinese export porcelain, and it became so popular that it was exported all over Europe. This fine collection shows the diversity and range of the many shapes and patterns that were produced.

Top left and top right
Always inexpensive and readily available, traditional shapes in white earthenware and stoneware have stood the test of time and are, quite rightly, as popular and practical today as they were hundreds of years ago.

Right
On a scrubbed pine table, the simple design of the rustic, patterned earthenware is set into relief by a starched runner. The combination is perfectly chosen.

Creamware was an immediate success and, in a relatively short time, Wedgwood added a royal seal of approval, re-christening it 'Queen's Ware' after he was awarded the endorsement of Queen Charlotte, wife of King George III. Further experimentation led to pearlware – even whiter, Wedgwood said, and soon to become just as successful as its predecessor.

It was also through the search for the perfect white that bone china – a type of porcelain that contained bone ash – was developed in England. In 1796–97, Josiah Spode made the first examples of bone china, which was remarkably white and fine. In 1812, Wedgwood made his version in a pure white that, unlike some earlier bone china, did not stain or craze. Today, bone china is still the standard British china.

Another well-known white body, made in America as well as England during the 19th century, was Parian ware (see pp.34–35), a sort of bisque porcelain that responded well to modelling and was used extensively for figures as well as moulded jugs and dishes. The Bennington pottery in Vermont produced Parian ware in all-white and also, occasionally, with blue backgrounds and white moulding, in the style of Wedgwood. Parian ware was also made in Trenton, New Jersey, where several potteries sprang up in the 19th century, as well as in Massachusetts, New York, Maryland and Ohio.

Today, many people admire and collect white ceramic ware, including porcelain, stoneware and earthenware. Although many types of white ware can never really be a true white (earthenware, for example, is too thick and porous), one of the joys of collecting these ceramics is to compare the nuances and tones of the different bodies and glazes.

Opposite
Moulded white earthenware by Astier de Villate is chosen by Véronique Lopez (see pp.130–31) for an enchanting table that could only be French; crescent-shaped floral garlands emphasise the floral design of the plates.

Above
Moulded designs have been employed since the early days of pottery-making, and are as popular today as they were then.

Below
This design is reminiscent of the garlanded and decorated dinner tables that were popular in Victorian England; it still works today because it introduces a pattern on the white surface without an excess of ornament.

coloured ceramics

Above
Variants on the popular blue and white china, such as this unusual soft lilac-blue, are much sought-after and can be hard to find.

Opposite (top left)
New York interior decorator Stephanie Stokes (see pp.124–25) uses a traditional colour scheme in a contemporary manner, arranging her 18th-century Chinese blue plates on a bright yellow and blue checked tablecloth, combined with 20th-century silver and glass.

Opposite (top right)
Blue and white china often looks best with other blue and white elements, here the table linen.

The early use of blue as a ceramic colour originated in China, as did most other colours; crushed cobalt was the pigment used because it was relatively available and could be easily applied under glaze. From the 14th century, the Chinese were producing blue on china, both for the domestic market and for export. In the early 17th century, a shipload of blue and white stoneware was auctioned in Amsterdam, causing a sensation and creating a vogue for Chinese blue and white china, which was collected throughout Europe by the wealthy. These early pieces of stoneware were then copied – at first in Delft in Holland and then in Bristol, Lambeth and Southwark in England, where this Dutch/English style of china became known generically as Delftware. Later, as the first pieces of delicate blue and white Chinese porcelain began to appear in the West, European potters experimented with various lighter ceramic bodies on which to use this winning colour combination, and by the mid-18th century, potters in France, Germany and England were producing hand-painted blue and white china designs on porcelain. The popularity of the blue and white combination was immense, particularly after the fashion reached a broader audience with the invention of transfer prints in the mid-1700s.

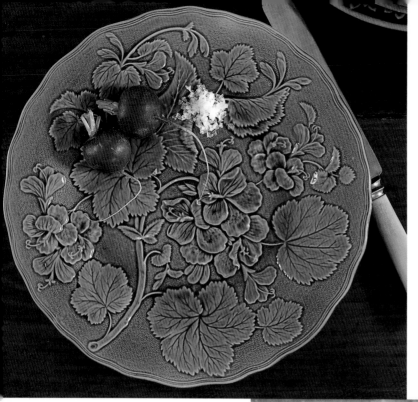

Simple colour ways like blue and white were not the only directions in which colour experimentation had been moving: from the time of the Renaissance, Europe (particularly Spain and Italy) had been creating ceramics that combined strong pigment colours with bold decoration, to make what was known as majolica (see pp.59–60). Italian Renaissance majolica painters experimented with different pigments to find out which would withstand firing at high temperatures, and discovered that turquoise, green-blue, brown and purple-black reacted particularly well.

By the 15th century, the Chinese were experimenting with enamel colours such as yellow, red and green, as well as subtle glazing methods. For many people, the delicate glazes the Chinese invented in the early 16th century have never been equalled. In the early 18th century, the Chinese introduced a new range of strong-coloured glazes specifically for Europeans, known as the 'Famille' colours (see p.64).

Meanwhile, there was a fledgling ceramic industry in Europe that was experimenting with its own strong and subtle pigments and glazes. Sèvres, the national porcelain manufacturer of France, developed new background

Above
Deep green plates, decorated with all-over relief patterns, were widely produced in the 19th century in both England and France, and are still produced today. The patterns are always leafy, often featuring a grapevine, but occasionally they illustrate foliage of other plants such as these strawberry leaves.

Right
A harlequin set of green leaf plates can be built up, using both old and new designs, and adding other small, leaf-shaped pieces to the mix. Here, glasses continue the theme, decorated with etched leaf designs.

Opposite
A plate with a green-glazed background from a 19th-century dessert service. These services were usually more elaborate than the dinner service, and were often kept on display, rather than stored, when not in use.

Right
Gilding has always been a popular form of decoration of formal dinner services, redolent as it is of status and wealth. Here, gilded service plates, on which dinner plates are placed, add glamour to every other element of the table.

Below
Tiny silvered ceramic goblets on a pewter cake stand work wonderfully with a traditional tea setting of white cups, which look almost shell-like with their scalloped edges.

Opposite
A modern take on gilding, where US interior designer Jamie Drake serves coffee in a brightly coloured contemporary set, which has the added distinction of being both gilded and lustred.

colours, which are today famous among all lovers of ceramics. Between 1749 and 1757, they introduced a wide range of distinctive shades, including dark blue or 'Gros Bleu', a turquoise known as 'Bleu Celeste', the vibrant pink 'Rose Pompadour', as well as yellow and apple green.

By the late 18th century, there was an energetic and imaginative ceramic industry in England. Although they continued to copy Chinese porcelain in design and pattern, they also experimented with different bodies and ways of creating new decorative finishes. In the vanguard, once again, was the entrepreneurial potter Josiah Wedgwood, who launched any number of innovative ceramic bodies, many of which are still made and bought today, including the unglazed, matt black stoneware named basalt (see pp.68–69), the hard red stoneware known as rosso antico, and the innovative jasperware, which is still the ceramic finish and body most closely associated with Wedgwood, not only in the famous, eponymous blue, but also in green, mauve and, surprisingly, yellow.

From the 18th century onwards, new pigments were discovered, many of them synthetic, and the range of colour made possible by mixing pigments was hugely increased. Bright colours were much admired at that time, and 19th-century English potteries were particularly keen to reproduce the colour of Japanese Imari ware (see pp.69–70). In contrast, brown also became very popular from the late 18th century, as epitomised by the earthenware and stoneware made at the Bennington factory, founded in Vermont in the late 18th century. The distinctive, 'trickled' brown effect is instantly recognisable (see p.23), and these pieces are very valuable today.

Gilding has been in and out of fashion over the centuries. The method used in the 18th century was to apply a paste of gold leaf and honey to the piece before lightly firing. Modern gilding is an amalgam of gold and mercury, and although it lasts longer than the gilding of two centuries earlier, it lacks the same soft tones, and perhaps some of the charm.

By the 19th century, lustred ceramics, in which a decorative metallic film was applied over the glaze, were also very popular. Lustre colour derived from gold, silver and copper, which gave those hues to a variety of wares including jugs, coffee pots, beakers, plaques and other decorative china.

china pattern

Since the first moment that clay was turned, people have augmented their creations by adding ornamentation. From simple geometric patterns and shapes scratched into the surface of the clay to finely painted figurative designs that illustrated the world around the artist, the decorative element of china has always been an integral part of the creation. The greatest sources of inspiration for ceramic design have been classical (both Greek and Roman) and, most importantly, oriental art forms.

Opposite
A piece of Thai Sawankhalok ceramic ware, possibly dating from the 18th century, which illustrates the enduring popularity of Eastern design. These dishes were stacked in the kiln, which explains the unglazed circle in the centre.

Just as the Chinese potteries influenced and led the development of different colours and glazes in ceramics (see pp.40–55), so did they influence most of the designs and patterns used by Western potters.

Around the 14th century, there was a vast difference between the quality of ceramic work produced in China and that made in England. In Chinese ceramics, hand-painted designs in blue glaze depicted, often with great skill and sensitivity, scenes from the natural world, including landscapes, wildlife, trees and flowers. In contrast, early English earthenware was decorated with fairly basic patterns, either slip-decorated or consisting of vaguely geometric designs scratched into the body of the clay before firing.

By the 15th century, in southern Europe, lead and salt glazing dramatically opened up design possibilities. Renaissance earthenware – particularly those pieces made in Italy and Spain, where they were influenced by the strong Moorish tradition of earthenware decoration – was bold and exuberant in pattern. Generally known as majolica (often

Both pages
Transfer-printed blue and white designs have possibly been the most successful patterns ever. The early Western designs were usually based, albeit vaguely, on Chinese subjects, particularly landscapes.

Later designs included Eastern or Western sporting activities (opposite), romantic, idealised landscapes (top left) and commemorative plates (top right and left), many of them printed for individual people or institutions.

pronounced 'maiolica'), these pieces show well-executed animals, birds, flowers, insects, men and gods as well as heraldic and armorial designs. Depictions of Bible stories or well-known legends were also common. On the whole, these pieces of majolica were made more as presentation or commemorative pieces than as dishes to be used on a daily basis.

Until about the 17th century, tableware fell into one of two extremes: the wealthy ate from silver plates, at least on high days and holidays, and everyone else

took their meat from relatively basic platters – first wood or pewter and later, in the 16th century, from tin-glazed earthenware. At first, the designs of this everyday earthenware were not very sophisticated, but by the 17th century, when the first pieces of imported Chinese porcelain arrived in Europe, potters in Europe turned their hands to copying the exotic Eastern ware. The rich took to this new fine ceramic material, while the less wealthy bought earthenware and stoneware, which were being produced in ever-greater quantities.

Above
Stephanie Stokes (see pp.124–25) uses blue and white in a clean, modern way; the plates are a Swedish neoclassical design.

Opposite
On the principle that more is more, Kate Dyson (see pp.126–27) uses varying blue and white designs, with mixed blue and clear glass, and an all-over embroidered blue and white cloth.

Opposite
This teacup and saucer (here, with an all-over design vaguely representing coral) are highly representative of literally thousands of designs produced during the late 18th and early 19th centuries by many now unknown Staffordshire potteries.

Left
A delightful collection of mainly blue and white ceramic ware from the 18th and 19th centuries, including hand-painted and transfer-printed pieces, a pair of chinoiserie hexagonal dishes and a cow creamer with striped tail and horns.

Below
Swedish interior designer Moussie Sayers, owner of the shop Nordic Style in London, mixes together antique blue and white pieces and modern pieces of tin-glazed ware from Isis Ceramics, inspired by the patterns and shapes of 17th-century English Delftware.

Chinese blue and white porcelain and earthenware swiftly became more than a fashion, almost a cult, and the phrase 'blue and white' no longer referred to a straightforward combination of colours but rather a style of design that was highly recognisable. The designs at this time all depicted idealised scenes of China – romantic, far-eastern landscapes, figures in oriental clothing, exotic flowers and plants – and it was this exotic element that so charmed the new Western buyers. As the export trade with Europe grew, Chinese craftsmen refined and extended the range of their designs, tailoring them more specifically to the lucrative European market, with themes and designs that they imagined to be Western in content. On their journeys to the East, the ships of the Dutch East Indian Company (the principal importers of Chinese porcelain, founded in the early 17th century) took with them commissions from grand European families for dinner services to be made in China, the patterns for which were chosen from special books of designs and which were very often based around some

motif or design personal to the commissioning family, such as their coat of arms, crest or a representation of their principal country estate.

To meet this new, more critical market, by the early 18th century the Chinese began to develop a greater sophistication of design, as well as a new range of stronger colours in which to execute them. This was known as the famous 'Famille' range, and included 'Verte', 'Rose', 'Noir' and 'Jaune'. Although the names appear to refer simply to the colour of the china, they were actually generic names that characterised particular designs as well as the shade: a 'Famille Rose' piece, for example, is one of several designs represented within the pink colour range, and is easily recognisable to the china enthusiast. The designs of the 'Famille' range were based on traditional Chinese motifs and were decorative and sweeping, painted with a new freedom and naturalism, and often enclosed in panels or cartouches within the design.

This refinement and delicacy of oriental porcelain was like nothing ever seen before in Europe, and it was little surprise that as well as working hard to develop new ceramic bodies that would match the beauty and desirability of Chinese porcelain, European manufacturers

Right
An unusually coloured lilac and white transfer print incorporates several of the motifs that were fashionable in the early 19th century, such as Greek urns and formal architecture.

Below
The pale lilac dresser blends harmoniously with the tones of the blue and white patterned china.

Bottom left
This Swedish cup and saucer, unusually in lilac and white, features a Stockholm scene.

Below
Lena Proudlock, an interior designer based in Gloucestershire, uses her antique lilac and white printed ware on a table painted lilac but mixed with linen of different blues and clear glass; the effect is clean and crisp.

Below
A rare transfer-printed plate, featuring an elephant in the centre, in a deep, purple-brown tone that is rarely seen in ceramics.

Above and right
Transfer-printed ware in green and brown tones – part of Peri Wolfman's impressive collection (see pp.136–37). Peri is so taken by this genre of ceramic that she is reproducing several of the patterns for US china company Williams-Sonoma. The patterns are representative of the many designs made in English potteries in the early 19th century and adapted to what they thought was American taste. Later, American potteries produced their own printed ware, often illustrating local beauty spots.

Left and bottom left
Stephanie Stokes (see pp.124–25) has a fine service of dark brown and white transfer-printed ware, known as 'Greek', produced by Spode around 1815. The design used some of the subjects depicted on Greek vases excavated in the early 19th century from Etruscan tombs near Naples. The china is combined with French wine glasses found in a Paris flea market.

Below
Against a dramatic dark brown wall hangs a collection of brown and white transfer-printed plates, finished with intricate pierced decoration. The dark wall throws the dishes into sharp relief.

Left and top right
Black and white is always a chic, sophisticated option. In the apartment of French designers, Michael Coorengel and Jean Pierre Calvagrac (see pp.122–23), the table has been set with Wedgwood's 18th-century black basaltware, which is decorated with neoclassical cameo relief, teamed with a new design, 'Century', created by Coorengel and Calvagrac for Puiforcat.

worked at copying Chinese designs; indeed, there are few early 18th-century European patterns that were not based on Chinese designs. However, in the course of the 18th century, both European and, later, American potters began to develop their own decorative vocabulary, still influenced by oriental designs but touched with a whimsical, fanciful air. Europeans knew very little about China, and ceramic art tended to portray elaborately costumed figures against a background of turreted buildings and fanciful birds and beasts. This style of art became known as chinoiserie and was the ceramic form of the decorative style that captivated the West in the 18th century, affecting every branch of decoration from furniture to textiles and culminating in John

Nash's fabulous Brighton Pavilion, built for the Prince Regent in the early 1800s.

Japan also made fine porcelain, with designs of great restraint and beauty, and skilfully coloured with an instantly recognisable range of tones (see pp.78–79). In the late 17th and early 18th centuries, pieces from both the Kakeimon and Imari potteries were imported into Europe; they were instantly admired and soon much copied by many, including the Meissen factory in Germany and the Chelsea works in England. Kakeimon porcelain is immediately recognisable – immensely subtle in design and colour, usually with a pure white background, decorated with delicate figures and symbols. Imari designs are in colourful contrast –

Left
French faience plates, depicting rural sporting pursuits, are hung down the centre of a bookcase.

Below and bottom left
Deep yellow glazed faience plate (below) and hand-painted faience pattern based on a traditional design (bottom left), both from Soleil studio in Moustiers, France.

strong designs that cover the surface of the piece, depicted in deep, rich tones. The dominant colours of both Imari and Kakeimon ware were reds, yellows, blues and turquoise, often highlighted with generous gilding. Around the 1740s, the Japanese withdrew from almost all contact with the Western world, preferring to remain culturally isolated, a position they maintained for over a century. In the 1850s, when they re-established Western contact, many pieces of traditional Imari were brought to the West; at the Paris Exhibition of 1867, the Japanese display caused a sensation, and ignited a fashion for all things Japanese. Once again, the two ceramic styles – simple and subtle Kakeimon, and luxuriant and ornamental Imari – were taken up by both buyers and European potters alike (see p.76). Royal Worcester, for one, enjoyed popular success following the exhibition with a highly individualistic interpretation of Japanese design – all angled forms and heavy gilding – and in the 20th century, richly decorated and gilded pieces, in the manner of Imari, were still being produced by potteries such as Royal Crown Derby.

Opposite
This plate is a good example of faience from Brittany in France. The pottery, known as Quimper after the town of its origin, is still made today and usually depicts the traditional dress and pastimes of the Breton people.

Another decorative style that was extraordinarily successful in ceramics was neoclassicism. In the mid-1700s, the educated world was fascinated by the ongoing excavations at the towns of Pompeii and Herculaneum in southern Italy; of particular interest were the ancient treasures, such as sculptures and vases, that were being brought up out of the earth. Designers were seduced by the lure of the classical and the purity of the design, and the neoclassical movement was warmly embraced by everyone from furniture-makers to glass-makers and potters.

The innovative potter Josiah Wedgwood (1730–95) was particularly inspired by the neoclassical movement. During his lifetime, he developed any number of new and different bodies; then he commissioned the most famous great artists and designers of the day – for example, the sculptor Joseph Flaxman and the great architect and furniture designer Robert Adam, a man equally inspired by the neoclassical movement – to create designs that would specifically enhance and beautify his revolutionary ceramic bodies. The resulting designs featured delicate representations of

Opposite
Stencilled designs and spongeware are two of the earliest forms of ceramic decoration and are much sought after today. Here, antique bowls have been mixed with new pieces such as those made by Emma Bridgwater, whose designs are widely available.

Above
Mottled glazes, often of several different shades, are an earlier form of decoration than complex figurative designs. This mottled plate was probably made in the early 19th century.

Right
A beautiful and unusual set of 19th-century Wedgwood creamware called 'Garden Implements'. Although rural in theme, this service was not originally designed for farming folk but for someone who 'played' at the country life.

the classical, from grotesques to architectural ornament, as well as delicate raised classical cameo designs, which stood out against the rich plain background of his jasperware and basaltware (see pp.68–69). One of the ceramic bodies that Wedgwood developed was creamware (see pp.45–49, 154–155). Although creamware is usually without additional pattern, relying simply on artistic techniques such as cutwork designs and using the shape of the piece itself to demonstrate the beauty of the white ceramic body, it responded equally well to applied decoration, and Wedgwood naturally used it as a background for the ever-popular neoclassical designs and motifs. This time, however, instead of hand-decorating the pieces, he employed the new, much simpler and less expensive transfer-printing technique.

Transfer printing was the decorative technique that transformed the pottery industry, bringing its wares to the many rather than the few. Developed in England in the 18th century, the method was to use a transfer, printed from an engraved copper plate onto tissue paper, which was then applied over the glaze or, from the 1780s, under the glaze, onto a piece of pottery. By the late 18th century, British potters had embraced the transfer-print technique with enthusiasm, among them Josiah Spode (1754–1827), who produced some of the best examples, often using the popular colour combination of blue and white. Although blue and white transfer-printed ware was the most widespread, other monochrome combinations also became popular – the perennially fashionable black and white and, later, purple, green and a warm brown or sepia (see pp.66–67).

Opposite
First produced in the 1920s and 1930s as tea sets, and sometimes called chintzware, these all-over floral patterns are still made today, and are widely available. It is fun to mix styles, not only different patterns, but also old and new together.

Right
A stylised gingko leaf adorns this set of china, which harmonises beautifully with the glass tumblers. The glass serving plates are part of the famous 'Point de Diamont' range, by Casa Lopez.

Bottom left and bottom right
A harlequin set collected by Kate Dyson of the Dining Room Shop (see pp.126–27). The theme is floral, and each plate – most of them pre-1840 – has a different central motif and coloured border. Although the plates come from several different sets, the generic style was popular enough in the 19th century to offer a wide range of patterns to choose from. Cranberry glass accentuates the rich Victorian colour.

The transfer patterns on much early blue and white china were copied from or based on oriental designs, the willow pattern being the most famous example of this. The willow pattern began life as a genuine Chinese design called 'Mandarin', which was a gentle land- and riverscape, typical of many such Chinese scenes; it was Spode who first added the other elements, such as the fence and the bridge with three figures running across it. It is interesting that it is these additions that gave the design its popularity,

subsequent potters varying everything from the number of figures on the bridge, to the number of trees and the shapes of the buildings. The willow pattern with all its many variants became so popular and sold so well that many people used the name to describe all blue and white pottery, whether or not it was inspired by Chinese designs.

By the 19th century, North America had become an important market and potteries in Staffordshire in England began exporting there, sending designs that

they hoped would appeal to their new customers (see p.66). Some were carefully executed renditions of American scenes or places, while others were existing designs that had simply been given an American name. The fledgling American ceramic industry, including manufacturers such as Bennington, Charles Cartlidge & Co. and Union Porcelain works, was soon making its own transfer-printed ware, many designs commemorating some of the momentous military events that were taking place at the time.

Another popular form of decoration since ceramics were first made has been relief-moulded and -decorated pieces. From the finest porcelain to sturdy stoneware or earthenware, potters have always delighted in adding an element of the third dimension – whether a simple moulded design of corn sheaves or grape leaves on an earthenware pitcher, or a fine and naturalistic rendition of a hand-painted spray of flowers or leaves on a porcelain plate. Other designs included small ornamental motifs such as ribbons, bows and flowers, or on larger dishes moulded vegetables and fruit, sometimes even animals or birds, which were often used to adorn a serving dish on which the specific creature might appear on the dinner table. Sporting and rustic motifs could be found on relief-decorated jugs,

Opposite
Japanese porcelain is collected by Nathalie Hambro (see pp.138–39), who appreciates the combination of both opulence and restraint in the designs. Set on a 1920s kimono, instead of a traditional cloth, this antique plate is unmistakably Imari ware.

Above
This heavily decorated and gilded plate illustrates the colour palette that has, for centuries, been distinctive to Japanese ceramics.

Left
These unusual rich, deep colours are influenced by the oriental palette. The combination of burgundies, greens and greys are set off by sang-de-boeuf (ox-blood) bud vases along the length of the table. The candlesticks are by Casa Lopez, the tablecloth by Pierre Frey.

Right
Part of crystal and furnishing designer William Yeoward's collection of early porcelain (see pp.120–21), featuring a pair of 19th-century Paris Porcelain plates (the origin of the central plate is unknown), a 19th-century pineapple stand and two unusual cups, one 18th-century Wedgwood creamware, with two handles.

Below
William Yeoward likes to combine ornate and decorated cut glass and fine porcelain on a background of a heavy oak table. This is a new design by William Yeoward, called 'Givalda', based on an antique design.

as well as pursuits enjoyed by the rural population, such as fox hunting, horse racing and – appropriately – drinking. The human form also features, as do classical themes. Designs of all kinds were often combined with inscriptions of various sorts – names, dates, bon mots, riddles and so on. Relief-moulded ceramics in a single colour – predominately green – became very fashionable, both in England and France, in the 19th century (see p.52). Also very popular and fashionable at this time was hand-painted faience ware, which was produced in France, Spain, Germany, the Netherlands and England. Today, this style of pottery survives as a peasant or rural art (see pp.70–71).

When considering the ongoing story of design and pattern in ceramics, it is evident that the close connection between fashion, interior decoration, architecture and ceramic decoration has always been present. In the early 18th century, the Rococo movement, for example, was well represented by ceramic form: the characteristic curves, asymmetry and serpentine swirls of Rococo lines were particularly suitable to malleable ceramic

This exotic, unusual arrangement, inspired by the decorative motifs of the French Empire in the early 19th century, is a striking combination of gilding and rich purples and blues. The setting consists of gold plates by Puiforcat, hand-painted porcelain teacups and purple crystal gilded glasses from the French glass company St Louis.

On William Yeoward's table is a place setting using new porcelain from his own range, called 'Gosford', based on the antique Paris Porcelain design in his collection (see opposite).

materials, and the designs showed themselves to advantage climbing over jugs, dishes, plates and pots. In the 19th century, Art Nouveau was well represented in ceramic decoration, and in the 20th century an artistic resurgence of the Stoke-on-Trent potteries led to many striking designs being created in Art Deco style by ceramic artists such as Susie Cooper and companies such as Shelley. Another form of Art Deco is represented by the works from Doulton, Carlton Ware and Clarice Cliff, and later designers, such as Eric Ravilious, brought 1950s graphic design to ceramics. The trend continues today, with vibrant, clear designs on strong-coloured backgrounds.

Interestingly, decorative ceramics, particularly earthenware, have frequently been used for political and propaganda purposes. The designs have sometimes been overtly political, with slogans and representations of popular political figures; in other cases, the messages have been more subtle or 'hidden', sometimes with a motif or slogan that could only be recognised by those who knew what they were looking for.

glass

Glass is one of the most mysterious of materials – it can be delicate, sheer and precious, yet it is also malleable, tough and highly adaptable. The very art of glass-making seems to have something magical about it: a combination of prosaic ingredients are mixed together, and then, when heated and blown into shape, turn suddenly into objects of beauty and surprise – some unadorned and simple, others decorative works of fragile art.

Opposite
Glass cake and fancy dishes have been popular since the 19th century; in this modern take on an old theme, three ever-decreasing dishes have been stacked one upon another, topped with a glass ice-cream dish, and filled with a selection of jewel-like bonne-bouches.

shape & function

Left
These coffee-coloured wine glasses, typical of the mid-20th century, are from various flea markets across the United States.

Opposite (top)
Designed for water and port, these 19th-century French glasses have ridged sides and heavy bases, which add to their charm.

Opposite (bottom left)
The classical tulip shape of this white wine glass not only looks good, but also allows wine to be enjoyed at its best (see p.86).

Opposite (bottom right)
For lovers of glass, all glass is of interest, whether low-stemmed or tall, square-based or rounded, cut or plain, decorated or simple.

The classical world was well acquainted with the beauty and versatility of glass; centuries before the birth of Christ, the Egyptians, Greeks and Romans all made glass vessels – bowls, jugs, flasks, bottles and dishes. Moulded or blown, imaginatively designed, and many of them spectacularly coloured and decorated, they were often deemed precious enough to be ceremoniously buried with their owners. Although in western Europe many of the techniques disappeared with the end of the Roman Empire, in the East, the Islamic world kept the glass-making tradition alive, embellishing what had gone before; it was this tradition, in turn, which inspired the Venetians to form their own glass-making industry. By the 14th century, Venetian glass was beautifully crafted and decorated, and it became the benchmark to which all other glass-makers aspired. It was exported across the world, and by the beginning of the 17th century, glass factories had been established in many other parts of Europe, where they made beautiful glass in the Venetian tradition.

Glass in all its beauty can – and should – be used as an integral part of the well-dressed table. William Yeoward (see pp.120–21) is an admirer of coloured glass and has here combined his own cranberry-coloured wine glasses and bowls with cut and decorated clear wine glasses, dramatic glass candlesticks and a simple glass water jug – all different in design, yet all in harmony.

In countries without a glass-making tradition, mostly in northern Europe, drinking goblets were made from pewter, horn or salt-glazed earthenware. By the 17th century, however, English glass-makers were successfully experimenting with making glasses out of a mixture that included lead oxide; these were heavier and sturdier than Continental glasses, but were more affordable. The popularity of this glass in northern Europe grew over the next two centuries as people moved towards drinking from individual glasses rather than communal ones.

The best drinking glasses are designed to enhance the colour, appearance and taste of the liquid within. White wine glasses are traditionally long-stemmed and narrow, to keep the white wine cool, while red wine glasses are rounder so that the bouquet may be savoured and the wine turned; traditionally, the glass is held by the bowl, which helps to warm the wine.

In the 18th century, glasses were brought to the table when requested, rather than being put into position at the place setting. However, by the 19th century a formal table arrangement would have had –

Left
New crystal, based on 18th-century designs; the glasses are weighty and satisfying to hold in the hand.

Below
The shape of a glass contributes greatly to the enjoyment of the drink. Wine glasses can have straight, rounded or angled sides.

Bottom left
Moulded glass was first developed as an alternative to cut glass, but was later admired as decorative in its own right (see pp.106–107).

literally – a line of different-shaped glasses before each place. In addition to various shapes of wine glasses and tumblers, there were glasses designed specifically for other drinks – for example, a narrow-bowled glass for ratafia (a fashionable liqueur) and a small-bowled, long-stemmed cordial glass. There were oddly shaped glasses, too – notably ones with footless stems, which obviously required to be finished in one gulp – these were the glasses of conviviality and toasts.

Individual wine-glass coolers (often now mistaken for finger bowls) were popular in the late 18th and early 19th centuries; designed like squat tumblers, the glass was left upside down in chilled water until required. Also produced at the time were communal wine-glass coolers – tureen-like dishes, with scalloped sides, into which the stem of the glass neatly fit while the bowl was immersed in chilled water.

By the mid-19th century, glass was being mass manufactured. This increased production meant that glass could be used for other household objects such as serving dishes and bowls.

Above and right
Wine jugs and decanters are
among the most satisfying of
glass forms and can be as simple
or decorative as personal taste
demands. Both antique and new
ones can be found in numerous
shapes from tall and elegant to
full-bottomed and practical.

Top right
Even when purely functional, glass
can also be decorative through
the simplicity of its design, as this
simple cream jug shows, based
on the traditional cream jugs used
in dairies.

Opposite
The joy of a collection of
decanters and carafes is that they
can be used to hold so many
other liquids as well as wine, thus
bringing increased enjoyment to
their owner. On the table a flat-
bottomed carafe holds cider, while
behind the sink a smaller version
holds washing-up liquid.

Right

Modern decanters are an opportunity for glass-makers to extol the sculptural qualities of glass in designing shapes that are as much pieces of art as functional objects. As with all good glass, contemporary design combines wonderfully with antique shapes. Coorengel and Calvagrac (see pp.122–23) combine new, cone-shaped carafes from the Conran Shop with traditional glasses by St Louis and Baccarat crystal candlesticks, all used with their contemporary design of china ('Voile') for Puiforcat.

Below

Véronique Lopez (see pp.130–31) successfully combines a selection of glass of different heights and styles, including candlesticks, tumblers and wine glasses that combine beautifully with the carafe in the 'Pointe de Diamont' design by Casa Lopez.

Bottles and containers have been made of glass since the technique of glass-making was first invented. Roman bottles can still be found in their numbers today, and the moulded glass bottles of the 19th century still survive in their thousands. Wine was kept in large casks until the 18th century and transferred into bottles to be served at table. The bottles were used countless times – until they broke – and the liquids within them were often distinguished by ceramic wine labels around the neck of the bottle.

By the 18th century, a dining table might have been dressed with silver, porcelain and decorative glass, so it was inevitable that the basic bottle would metamorphose into the decanter, which could hold its own in such rarefied company. Decanters came in many different shapes that were both varied and beautiful – round, square, cruciform and club-shaped, as well as the shape known as a 'ship's decanter', with its wide-bottomed base designed to keep the container stable in rough seas; what all these designs had in common was a large amount of surface area, so that when the wine-filled decanter was placed in ice, the liquid could be rapidly

Right
Dark glass is highly dramatic. Here, smoky grey glasses and an unusual carafe, like an inverted tulip, both Danish, set off Art Deco cutlery and silver and black china and objects.

Below
From the mid-18th century, decanters were often designed with full necks to act as a handle, with collar rings to give a sure grip. Decanters were originally made to be sold in pairs, so single antique pieces can be found relatively easily.

cooled. A sophisticated variation of this would be to embellish the straight body of the decanter with deep, fluted moulding, which would maximise the available surface area and increase the decanter's cooling capacity even more. Decanters might also be cut – sometimes very heavily – in order to reflect the light from the candlesticks. A table laid with the full complement of decanters, glasses and many-branched candlesticks must have been a dazzling, sparkling sight. If the decanter were of coloured glass, it might have an integral engraved gilded label; otherwise, a ceramic or silver wine label would be used.

Decanters were usually made in pairs or as sets of three. Fashion does not favour the decanter at the moment, so beautiful antique decanters may quite easily be found, particularly single pieces, in all their decorative guises. Many old decanters to be found today are sold without their original stoppers, which will have been lost or broken over time; although these are not of course totally complete, they will still suit their original purpose and are certainly worth buying.

The art of cut glass (see pp.102–103) was well illustrated in the design and making of chandeliers, which by the 18th century had become wonderful examples of the glass-cutter's skills. These chandeliers were often designed as the centrepiece of a matching group of lights, which would include standing table candelabra as well as glass wall lights that together lit up the room in spectacular fashion. With their glass garlands and ribbony strings of glass beads and faceted pendant drops, these candelabra, which might hold two or four candles, were a simpler and less expensive way of achieving some of the sparkling effect of the chandelier, and attractive antique examples can still be found today. But candelabra are, by their nature, ornate and do not suit every table or style. Glass candlesticks, bought as a pair or as single examples, are often easier to find than candelabra, and may be more suitable for a simpler table setting.

Candlesticks of either clear or coloured glass can be used on a table in a group, and are particularly effective – both from an aesthetic and practical point of view – if they are of varying heights and styles.

Above
This elongated glass candlestick would look as much at home in a traditional setting as it does in this contemporary spot. Its silver neck is an unusual feature.

Right
William Yeoward (see pp.120–21) combines different styles of glass candlesticks on a table with a pair of classical silver sticks. The decanters have been chosen to complement the chunky design of the candlesticks.

Opposite
An elegant take on the traditional hurricane light, so called because the tall glass sides would keep the candle from becoming extinguished in a strong wind. To vary the height of light at the table, they are combined with more traditional candlesticks. The attractive tablecloth is a Pierre Frey design.

coloured glass

The art of making coloured glass goes back thousands of years. In Ancient Egyptian times, it was sufficiently treasured for examples of coloured glass inlays to have been placed in the tomb of Tutankhamun. The techniques travelled through time and across continents, and by the time of the Roman Empire, coloured and gilded glass was made in quantity and was highly prized. Islamic glass-makers extended the techniques, and Islamic glass made between the 5th and 8th centuries was often highly coloured and ornately gilded.

Over the last five hundred years, coloured glass has enjoyed passing phases of popularity. Although Venetian glass was made in many colours as well as clear or opaque glass, until the end of the 18th century coloured glass was not much made in England. At this time, however, green became a popular colour for white wine glasses, as well as for wine bottles, probably because the liquid within would then look cooler than it actually was. Red and blue were also made, the red known as ruby or cranberry, and ranging from pale to very deep in tone. The blue shade is popularly called Bristol blue, although glasses in this deep shade were made in many other centres as well.

By the 19th century, colour was far more generally used – more so in Europe than in England. Colours were often vibrant in tone and sometimes applied in layers, which could be cut

Opposite
The glory of coloured glass is its adaptability and ability to add warmth and richness to a table; try mixing glass of more than one colour, as here, and combine it with china of an equally deep hue.

Left
Coloured glass indicates warmth and hospitality; there is a celebratory air about it, particularly when the glasses are as pretty as these pink floral tumblers.

Right
In this purple and green composition, many different designs of glass have been used, from old Victorian tea light holders, often used in the garden, to modern tumblers and sturdy carafes. The embroidered lilac cloth binds every element of the setting together.

Below
There is so much choice of coloured and decorative glass available today that lateral thinking brings the best results. Here, on a mirror-mosaic table, turquoise, pink and gold glass are combined for a rich, almost oriental, effect.

through in intricate fashion. In France, opaline glass became popular – this, as the name implies, was semi-translucent and milky like an opal, sometimes displaying refracted light within the glass; not only was it made in white, but also in tones such as blue-turquoise and soft pink-lilac.

Also developed at the beginning of the 19th century was a technique that gave glass the appearance of coloured marble. Called Lithyalin, it was produced in various shades – from a dark red to layered greys, purples and so on; another equally striking technique that developed around the same period was a method of producing a dramatic, solid black glass known as Hyalith.

Gilding, too, has seen its popularity wax and wane. In the 18th century, English glass-makers, unlike their Continental counterparts, used little gilding on their glassware, one of the reasons being that the fine clear glass that English glass-makers had perfected in the late 17th century was not the best background for gilded decoration, which is more effective when used with coloured glass. By the 19th century, however, coloured glass became fashionable, and more gilding was therefore employed.

Right
Distinctive antique French gilded and decorated glasses, together with similar, highly decorated wine jugs, form part of a collection of 19th-century glass. A rich turquoise background accentuates their decorative qualities.

Below
Gold decoration on glasses was only ever for the wealthy; it adds a feeling of instant opulence to a table, as illustrated by these St Louis purple crystal glasses, offset with gold cutlery and a gold candelabra. Both the utensils and the candelabra are re-editions by Puiforcat of 18th-century designs.

Overleaf (p.98)
Glass plates are not only an inexpensive way of setting a table, they also add a very interesting decorative element. Here, a glass plate in the same colour tones as the background cloth invites the eye to re-assess the usual and the obvious. Alternatively, contrasting-coloured glass is also effective.

Overleaf (p.99)
This striking, almost organic dish, commissioned by Nathalie Hambro (see pp.138–39) from Anthea Wilson, has an unusual pewter finish.

Left
Glass has been engraved for
centuries, using a number of
different methods. Leaves have
always been a popular motif –
sometimes, like grapevines, used
to indicate purpose (a wine glass,
for example), or simply as a
charming decorative feature, as
illustrated in the ferns used on
these tumblers.

Below
In the late 18th and early 19th
centuries, short-stemmed glasses
such as these were popular. They
were often highly decorated, either
with engraving or enamelling.

Opposite
Coloured stems on drinking
glasses were popular in the late
19th and early 20th centuries,
particularly in Europe. Combined
with etched decoration, they make
a good basis for a collection.

By the mid-18th century, glass that had been decorated with engraved
patterns was to be found on many tables. The methods, which tested the
skill of the engraver, included wheel-engraving with small copper discs, or
acid-etching. The numerous designs were varied, imaginative and
beautiful. Like so many of the ancillary arts attached to glass-making,
many of the surface-decorating techniques, including engraving, were first
developed by the Romans.

The widely used copper-engraving technique is particularly skilful: the
scene or inscription is sketched onto the glass by the engraver, who holds
a glass beneath a rotating wheel of metal or stone. The wheel slices a
series of facets through the surface of the glass with the assistance of
lubricating oil and an abrasive powder such as emery.

Acid-etching is a relatively easier and slightly less expensive process,
where acid-resistant wax is painted onto a glass and a design is then
incised through the surface of the wax. Acid is then applied to the object,
and cuts through into the glass where the wax has been scratched away,
leaving a design in these areas only.

textured glass

Opposite
in the 18th century, sets of heavily cut table glass were very fashionable, the aim being to create a fairytale effect with the light of the candles on the table reflected from the many facets of the assembled drinking glasses. Cut stems were also an important element of these glasses.

Left
As well as being decorative, the engraving of glass also served a practical purpose – that of identifying the owner. These modern Swedish glasses, from Nordic Style in London, are gilded and hand-engraved in the style made popular in the reign of Gustav III, in the 18th century.

Below
Beautiful antique champagne flutes, possibly 19th century and European, are beautifully engraved with a noble cipher.

Cut glass – in which the surface of the glass is sliced into a geometric design rather than engraving a picture into it – became fashionable at the end of the 18th century, although it had been practised as an art since the early 1700s. The skill employed in cutting glass was considerable, and the end result could often be very elaborate; in the same way that facet-cut glass reflected the candlelight, this early cut glass, on a candlelit table, would have appeared a shimmering fantasy. As cut glass gained in popularity, it became used for jugs and decanters as well as salad bowls, tall-stemmed celery glasses, flute-shaped vases, rose bowls and salts.

The English and Irish were the masters of glass-cutting – Irish cut glass, with its characteristic slightly grey-tinted tone, is highly collectable today – and by the 1800s the skills of the master craftsmen were imported to the rest of Europe, where they were in great demand. The designs were complex, consisting of graduated diamonds and sharp-edged fluting that reflected the light. Such elaborate designs gradually became less fashionable, and by about 1830 a new, simpler style was beginning to become popular, consisting of plain vertical facets or pillars cut into the glass – a sharp contrast to the ornate patterns of earlier years.

Opposite
New glass is the old glass of tomorrow. Swedish interior designer Moussie Sayers uses new Swedish glass at her shop Nordic Style, in London, featuring designs that are classical yet contemporary (see plate, right).

Right
Modern glass plates, both plain and decorated, are inexpensive and widely available. A large-sized glass service plate is an interesting alternative to a table mat and adds depth without mass to any plates used on top of it, whether ceramic or glass.

Left
Old etched glass is generally easy to find. The theme of this collection, ranging from the mid- to late 19th century, is decorative leaves rather than shape – each style has a border or motif of leaves. Many people now collect etched glass from the early 20th century rather than the 19th century as it is less expensive; single pieces are always cheaper to buy than pairs or sets.

Moulded glass – so universally popular by the 19th century – was, by the nature of its semi-industrial process, less expensive to make and therefore to buy than hand-blown and shaped glass. The glass could be moulded into shape in two ways – it was either blown directly into a mould, or was pressed as molten glass into the mould using a plunger. The first method was ancient, and originally used by the Romans and the Venetians, the second began to be used in the 19th century, in parts of Europe and particularly in the United States. The American glass-making companies made the process their own, using the widest possible variety of designs, patterns and colour and the highest standards of manufacture. As the makers' skills grew, the variety of shapes that could be

Above
By the 19th century, metal moulds were used to produce every shape of bottle and glass, a commercial process that went on into the 20th century. The wide range of colours produced (some of which are shown here) mean that it is not difficult to put together a harlequin set.

Right
Depth and contrast of texture are what is fascinating about glass; here, a jug copied from an antique Venetian design is grouped with swirled tumblers and smooth glass pebbles by Giorgia Vigna.

Left
A table set with nothing but glass – except for the cutlery – is an interesting exercise in light and shade. Because only glass is used, it is important to vary the texture and decoration of the pieces. The underplates are modern American, the decorative plates on top are Victorian, and the tumblers are modern Italian.

Below
Instead of using glass plates on a coloured background, it is more interesting, if a trifle unsettling, to use a neutral base. This table has a brushed steel finish, known as 'scuffed', which plays with and reflects the light.

achieved increased. Everything that could be was made in pressed glass. Patterns varied from simple geometrics to intricate and complex multi-faceted designs, and it was especially popular for commemorative ware.

Pressed moulded glassware could be clear or coloured, both in luminous shades and opaque ones such as milk-white, strong turquoise and deep blue, all of which became very popular for many years. Pressed glass could also be produced in a semi-translucent, opaline finish as well as in dramatic Hyalith solid black and Lithyalin marbled effects (see p.96). Another striking finish was iridescent glass, originally developed to partly emulate the different lustreware glazes then so popular in ceramics (see p.55). Most often known as carnival glass, the pieces have a bronzed rainbow effect, a finish that looks a little like scattered drops of petrol in a puddle, and it is much collected in the United States today. Other 20th-century glass from America includes 'Depression glass'; made during the Depression years of 1929–39, it was mass produced in large quantities and was correspondingly cheap. Many factories produced it, and there was a wide selection of colours from red, black and white to blue, pink, green and yellow.

using china & glass

the art of the table

Dressing a beautiful and well-appointed table is an art in itself and is to be much admired. Historically, as more and more people began to acquire the items required to present an imposing table – the china, the glass, the silverware and, of course, the decorations – it became expedient to show off all these new and often valuable belongings, displaying the host's exquisite taste and riches. The well-dressed table became as much an object of status as of style.

Previous page
In this dining room, overlooking the River Thames, blue and white is used on everything from plates to cushions. The blue and white theme is employed with charm and restraint.

Opposite
Whether a table is formal or informal in style, it should look welcoming. This table, in the apartment of New York interior decorator Jamie Drake, perfectly combines sharp style with traditional taste.

Traditionally, the main decorative focus of the table was the centrepiece, which might be a single piece or a decorative tableau. The emphasis on the centrepiece had developed, in part, from the importance attached in the Middle Ages to the salt cellar, originally just called the 'salt' – the dish or container used to hold the valuable and highly prized condiment. At medieval banquets, the seating arrangements were very precise: the precious salt container was placed at the lord's end of the table, and above it sat those who were deemed equal in status to their host; lesser personages sat further down, below the salt. During the Renaissance, the salt could be a work of art in its own right – for example, the famous dish made by the great Florentine goldsmith, Benevenuto Cellini, for King Francois I of France in the 1540s; this was an exquisite golden vessel enriched with enamel depicting, allegorically, the meeting of sea and land to produce salt.

Some centrepieces were less formal, and occasionally included whimsical elements. In the late 17th century, there was a widespread fashion for elaborate centrepieces made from sugar paste; these were made with great skill and were extraordinarily detailed, depicting figures, buildings, animals and landscape features such as trees and lakes. By the early 18th century, however, these sugar-paste figures had been replaced by ornamental porcelain ones. The Meissen factory in Germany, for example, made a centrepiece that included figures, farmhouses, barns and stables, all to be arranged in bucolic charm along the length of the table; this design was later copied by the English potteries. In addition to porcelain, other materials were also used for these conceits – follies and figures, pagodas and people could be found in enamelled glass, silver gilt and even gilded cardboard. If purchase seemed too expensive an option, such tableaux could even be hired. The idea of the table landscape

Left
Simplicity is often more appealing than an excess of richness. This elegant table, in the New York apartment of interior decorator Anthony Cochrane, is laid with almost minimal style in keeping with its surroundings. Nothing is over-emphasised; everything is subtle.

Right
A plainly polished table top is the background for simple china and glass, a story of neutrals from white to coffee-brown. Beneath a large white service plate, a generously sized napkin acts also as an instant table mat. Unusual coffee-coloured glass completes the sketch.

Left
The shapes of plates, dishes, glasses and silver on a table are tremendously important, for it is they as well as the colours that add interest, particularly when there is a sharp contrast in form.

Bottom left
An antique formal set of dessert plates is put out on a French country table of cherry wood. The elaborate objects combined with the rustic furniture offer a pleasing contrast in styles.

Bottom right
This sophisticated picture in contrast and colour is inspired by tables in the Far East, particularly Japan, where a combination and variety of different plate shapes have long been appreciated.

Opposite
There is something immensely satisfying about the country table, simply set with the wherewithal for a fulfilling meal.

remained popular for many years. James Woodforde, the greedy 18th-century English parson who kept a fascinating diary, described a dinner in 1783 with the Bishop of Norwich, on whose table was placed 'the most beautiful artificial garden – a yard long – with temple and pillars, shepherd and shepherdess'.

As time went on, the actual arrangement of the dinner table became more and more elaborate. By the 19th century, as can be seen in paintings of the time, the formal banquet table was a sight to behold, with scarcely an inch of polished table or starched tablecloth left uncovered by the things thought necessary to the feast. Quite apart from the actual place settings, which in themselves were fairly comprehensive and extensive, there would be an assortment of ornamental serving dishes and bowls as well as various ornaments such as silver-gilt palm trees or animals, elaborate candleabra, showy flower arrangements, garlands down the sides of the cloth, and often a lavish 'epergne', which was a salver or salvers, often in silver or glass, raised on branches and holding tasty sweetmeats and fruits.

By the 20th century, except for the most formal of banquets, the setting of a table had become considerably simpler; so much so that in some quarters it had developed into a very dreary arrangement indeed. It had become fashionable for formal dinner services to be ordered complete with matching dinner plates, side plates, bowls, serving plates and covered dishes – dull indeed; we seemed in many ways to have lost the sense of harmony between dish and food, of a pleasing presentation – something which the Japanese, with their centuries of a strong aesthetic tradition, have always understood.

In Japan, the presentation of even simple foods is carefully thought about; strawberries, for example – a great delicacy and available only for a short season – are always served on a black or dark green dish, such a dark colour showing off the red fruit to perfection. The best restaurants in Japan keep whole sets of dishes and utensils to be used in specific and particular seasons – autumnal dishes favour reds, golds, browns and black; in summer, food is often served on decorative glass to suggest a frosty coolness, and spring dishes might be served on a dish moulded into

Opposite
Irish writer and stylist Trish Foley is a great collector of all things white – at least where china is concerned. She combines shape and texture and all different shades ranging from pearl-white to porridge-brown.

Above
Traditional Scandinavian style is elevated to a particular sophistication, where a lilac painted table top is echoed by surrounding lilac woodwork. The china is blue and white, as are the seat cushions and the linen.

Right
Breakfast Scandinavian style – a sophisticated version from Swedish interior designer Moussie Sayers of the Nordic Style shop in London. There is no need for a cloth as the surface of the table has been painted with a blue on white pattern that picks up the attractive design of the china (called 'Ostindia').

Right

Comfort and grandeur are combined in this setting for coffee: old glass, silver and white china are set against rich taffeta and period furniture.

Opposite

The combination of rattan chairs and gilded plates is an interesting one, and creates a look that French interior decorators Michael Coorengel and Jean Pierre Calvagrac (see pp.122–23) admire. The 'Fantasy' candlesticks are designed by them, the decanters are Art Deco and the black basaltware bowls were made by Wedgwood.

the shape of a blossom. The material of the container or plate is also a matter for consideration: will the dish be shown at its best on wood, pottery, porcelain or bamboo? And then the shape – would a geometric shape be best, or something in the shape of a leaf or a fish? And finally the colour and glaze – dark and lacquered, pale and delicate, plain or with a subtle design? It will all depend on the dish to be presented, the time of year and the required final effect.

The vast selection of new china and glass available today and the wide variety of old pieces still to be found mean that those with an eye and style can create table settings every bit as interesting as those of our forebears, both in the East and the West. Today, the inspiration behind the best table designs is, broadly, based on one of three elements – colour, shape or

texture – all used with a freedom and lack of conventional ideas that would have been astonishing 50 years ago. Almost none of the tables in this book, for example, relies on using only one pattern of china or glass – styles are mixed with what seems like abandon (although they are actually very carefully thought out and executed) and colour is used to interest and even excite. In the same way that an unusual group of objects or a collection is arranged with care, so the most interesting tables are dressed to give pleasure before you begin to eat. Sometimes cloths or other types of textiles are used, sometimes not, but in the cases where they are used, they are as much part of the overall design as the china or glass. Flowers or plants may be included; alternatively, the table may be devoid of other decoration, relying instead on the composition of the dishes and utensils.

the formal table

For many people, the dressed table is synonymous with formality. The host or hostess may want their table to look special for a dinner party, and feel that a formal look is all that will do, particularly if they own antique china or glass. The most important aspect in dressing a formal table is discipline, order and harmony, which should always be present throughout.

William Yeoward

William Yeoward has played a great part in reviving the tradition of fine English glass and introducing to a new generation of glass-lovers the joys and beauty of English crystal. A few years ago he began to reproduce some of his personal collection of antique glasses, basing his contemporary ranges on some of the most beautiful and definitive designs of the past.

William has always extolled the virtues of coloured glass – long before it came back into fashion; there is both blue and cranberry glass in his range, and he feels, rightly, that coloured glass gives a depth and a resonance that clear glass cannot provide. When combining china and glass, he groups them both by shape and colour, but the colour does not have to be limited to a single shade. If several colours are present – for example in a complex china design – he suggests picking one colour (preferably the least obvious) and using that as a keynote.

Opposite

In his Gloucestershire kitchen, William Yeoward combines the formal and the intimate with the off-beat. A table laid for a weekend lunch is replete with crystal glasses, porcelain tableware, and tall glass pineapple holders.

Left

With its range of shades from rich ruby-red through to deep amethyst, cranberry glass has been collected since the 18th century. Here, it is used on a dark oak background with pale plates and a small bouquet of deep red roses.

Coorengel & Calvagrac

Michael Coorengel and Jean Pierre Calvagrac are two of Paris's most assured young interior decorators and designers. For them, formality is a way of life; that is not to say that they are formal in their manner – far from it – but their favoured style is the classical, both the art of antiquity and the neoclassical as admired in the early 19th century. When describing the source of their inspiration and designs they say: 'We love the neoclassical as an interpretation of what has gone before, and what is balanced and harmonious with the past. As designers we are sensitive to these balances.' They are also interested in what one might call the new classics – contemporary pieces that share the same stylistic influences as their predecessors; indeed, they design contemporary pieces, which they 'hope will have a past in the future . . . perhaps they will themselves become classics.'

Coorengel and Calvagrac collect china and glass and, not surprisingly, their taste there also runs to the classical – mixed with a generous measure of gilding, both on china and glass, using both single pieces and entire sets to glimmer and shine on their tables.

Above
Michael Coorengel and Jean Pierre Calvagrac have always espoused a style that links the richness of the neoclassical with the contemporary. Here, in the White Room, the heavy carved table is set with a combination of black and white china, designed by these two talented designers for Puiforcat, with antique basaltware by Wedgwood.

Right
Another combination of the ancient and modern in the Blue Room: an almost abstract china pattern, designed by Coorengel and Calvagrac for Puiforcat, set off with modern carafes from the Conran Shop, an Art Deco glass teapot and Art Deco cutlery from Puiforcat.

Coorengel and Calvagrac are great admirers of colour, so much so that each of the rooms in their apartment is colour-coordinated. There is the Terracotta Room, the Blue Room (see opposite, bottom right) and the dramatic Black Room, as well as the very sophisticated White Room (see opposite, top left), which is a study in neutrals – the colours range from French grey to charcoal to unpainted plaster – all very classical. The Mauve Room (see left and below), all in purple and red, is a mixture of East and West, and contains Chinese lanterns and other exotic elements. In every room, the function of the colour that they use on the walls is to blend all the pieces in that room together, giving all the objects a greater intrinsic value: 'The colour is important; the function of colour here is to blend everything together; it helps to unite pieces of varying quality.' Their vision is so focused that there is never a clash between styles and objects.

The pieces that Coorengel and Calvagrac design for the French china company Puiforcat (see opposite) are equally strong in colour terms, and they prefer to show them mixed with the old, in order to demonstrate the continuity of design and of colour history. It is, they say, about relating shapes and objects, about harmony and balance.

Above

A room dominated by brocades, damask and deep, rich, early 19th-century colour is the setting for this evocation of dinner with La Traviata. The glasses are purple and gilded crystal, made by St Louis; the gold plates are produced by Puiforcat, as are the candelabra and centrepiece, both replicas of 18th-century designs; the hand-painted teacups and plates are Le Tallec Limoges porcelain.

Right

In the Coorengel/Calvagrac apartment, each room is of a different colour and unique decorative style. This is the Mauve Room, and the theme here is rich and sumptuous with an oriental flavour.

Stephanie Stokes

One of New York's top decorators, Stephanie Stokes is through and through a formal diner. It isn't that her dinners are formal in themselves, it is that she thinks in formal terms when arranging a table: harmony of colour and shape is important, as is the background, particularly the tablecloth. Take the blue glass she collects – on one table she will combine candlesticks, water glasses, a decorative centrepiece and single blossom vases, all in blue glass, although four quite different styles; as a background, she uses a pale blue cloth that is neither too strong, nor too similar. It works because there is an understood order within the scheme.

Stephanie collects all types of china and glass, from 17th-century Chinese earthenware to Baccarat crystal, and she uses it all. 'I couldn't care less where anything comes from as long as it's pretty, and the right scale and colour,' she says. Her skill is using all her pieces in the right combinations. Because she buys what she likes when she sees it, she doesn't have any large, matching sets of china. In fact, she sometimes changes the colour with each course, so colour is not necessarily a constant theme throughout the dinner.

Above
Stephanie Stokes uses her Manhattan apartment as a setting for entertainment and pleasure. Against a fine antique mirror and a group of rich-toned Chinese pots, she sets antique Chinese earthenware dishes and combines them with green glass, an informal checked cloth and a brass bowl full of autumnal chrysanthemums.

Right and opposite
Around a centrepiece of a mirrored lazy Susan and ornamental pieces of 20th-century spun blue and white glass is set a table of blue and white sophistication: Scandinavian plates, a neoclassical design, are mixed with 19th-century Tiffany silver, blue and white Swedish tumblers and gilt-rimmed clear wine glasses. Blue glass bulb vases are filled with single orchid blooms.

the informal table

The informal table is the one at which most of us sit on an everyday basis. The prerequisites of the genre are an easy charm, a grouping of pretty and useful china and glass and, above all, an air of comfort and ease.

Kate Dyson

There is nowhere better than Kate Dyson's Aladdin-like shop in Barnes in London in which to see the art of the table, for gathered together in the Dining Room Shop is every manner of china, glass, cutlery and other pretty pieces, both old and new, grouped together in original and inspirational arrangements, many of them mixing patterns and colour. Kate Dyson is thought of as the inventor of the harlequin set – she is certainly a persuasive advocate of the style: 'I am very anti everything matching –

which is not to say that there should not be a link between pieces; a set has to be cohesive, to relate in some way, either in colour or in pattern, or even a single element within a pattern.'

A favourite scheme of Kate's is using blue and white china, which she feels is best mixed together in profusion: 'The glory of blue and white is that you can combine good antique pieces with car boot sale finds, as well as with reproduction designs and new pieces and it will all work together. In fact, the more designs and shapes used, usually the better it works. Any two-toned china, in fact, can be mixed with other pieces in the same genre.' Kate has two pieces of advice on the art of laying a fine table: 'Don't be over-ambitious; keep it simple and it will work' and 'Soldierly precision as you lay – the nicest things in the world are useless unless they are arranged with care.'

Opposite

The delights of al fresco dining at its most seductive are brought home in Kate Dyson's London garden; in a trellis-hung pergola, a table is set with all that is best for a long, informal summer lunch. An earthenware jug is filled with high-summer flowers.

Right

To match the emphatic colours and shapes of garden life (see opposite), the table is covered with a cheerful checked cloth on which are laid colourful decorative tin plates, ornamented with designs taken from antique porcelain dishes. On top are deep green English majolica plates with moulded floral patterns, and green glass tumblers complete the verdant setting. A 19th-century green majolica compote is filled with raspberries.

Left and below
At home, Victoria prepares simpler food than in her restaurant, yet she still takes care with its presentation: each dish is set on exactly the right piece of earthenware for its colour, texture and taste. Victoria favours faience from the Soleil studio in Moustiers in the South of France.

Opposite
For a country brunch, much thought has been given to the combination of textures, colours and shapes: twists of charcuterie and fruit on an oval platter, fat olives in a deep bowl and round amuse-bouches in a square dish, all illustrate the connection between platter and food. The cheery sunflowers give a feeling of endless summer sunshine.

Victoria du Roure

Victoria du Roure is an outstanding cook – her hotel and award-winning restaurant, Home Hill in New Hampshire, which she co-owns with her French husband Stephane du Roure, is among the best restaurants on the east coast of the United States and is a member of the highly regarded French Relais et Chateaux group. Victoria believes in simplicity and taking great care in choosing and using china and glass. In the restaurant, beautiful white china, commissioned from Bernadout in Limoges, is used.

The food that she cooks and the dish on which it is served are carefully matched: 'At the risk of sounding pretentious, one cannot underestimate the importance of the right shape and the right container for the right food. The way that I do it is to come up with the menu first, and then spend a whole day going around looking at the china and just figuring out what will go in what shape. That's the fun of it.' A thick green soup, for example, might be served in the depths of a deep white bowl, the green luminous against the white (see p.45). At home, however, a more informal mood prevails. Here, traditional French faience in that inimitable warm, food-loving yellow is the preferred china.

Véronique Lopez

Véronique Lopez operates a successful press relations agency in Paris, promoting the finest luxury goods as well as her own particular brand of *art de vivre*. Her list of prestigious clients is as impressive as her long association with the most prominent manufacturers, not least Pierre Frey, Wedgwood and Roche Bobois.

Together with Bernard Magniant, founder of Casa Lopez and specialist in needlepoint accessories, Véronique has created these beautiful rooms in one of her Paris apartments. The rooms have been furnished in understated but timelessly elegant detail, and the tables are dressed with the most stylish and beautiful china and glass.

Véronique's style is a fascinating mixture of everything that is modern and informal while being traditional and distinctly French. There is a simplicity in her tables, and yet an artfulness; colour is almost monochrome, but her arrangements are enlivened with interesting, yet simple additions – always within a particular colour palette. Despite the lack of bright colours, her tables are anything but dull – the textures and tones make it visually satisfying and remarkably welcoming.

Opposite
Véronique Lopez has a very distinctive and instinctive French understanding of how to make the simplest of food look good. At the side of the room, an old French painted buffet is piled high with desirable dishes – the different ingredients being served in containers that complement them. The whole buffet has been made into a tableau about, and for, the pleasure of food.

Above and right
The colour at Véronique Lopez's table comes from the food; the setting is just that, a subtle and sophisticated background that does not compete. Tones of grey, green and lightly glazed white are the predominant shades. The beautiful plates are by Wedgwood and Astier de Villate.

the contemporary table

It is wonderful that the art of table setting is not only not dead, but it has become rejuvenated with the renewed interest in ceramic and glass design. Once again seen as a legitimate decorative art form, the choice and diversity of contemporary design is vast.

Dominique Lubar

An integral part of the design partnership with London-based François Gilles, Dominique Lubar is a great exponent of clean-cut, simple and interesting modern design. She spends much of her time in France, where she hunts for pottery to add to her collection, particularly French pieces of the mid-20th century, up to the 1960s: 'It was very different from English pottery of the period, and to my mind, far more sophisticated and interesting, both in shape and design.' She currently seeks out Capron, a manufacturer that produced intricate designs incorporating many tiny squares of colour. She is not immune to the charms of old porcelain, but remains patriotic, preferring French pottery.

Opposite and left
Dominique Lubar understands the art of contemporary table settings. Fiercely dramatic square plates, designed by Pablo Picasso, are laid on top of deep, square black dishes, which highlight the drama of the Picasso design. Instead of a conventional tablecloth, she uses two long runners – one either side of the table – to ground the place settings and acting as a dramatic contrast to the dark plates. Glasses, some with coloured stems, others of an all-over pattern, hold their own against the strong-edged plates.

Reem Acra

Reem Acra, New York-based designer of sophisticated wedding dresses, has a particular decorative style that combines a contemporary understanding of ceramics and glass with an Eastern sensuality and a love of rich textures and colour. She skilfully combines the striking and the unusual in an approachable and innovative way. In her apartment, for example, Reem uses mirrored tables, and against this fractured, reflective background she sets china and glass in mauve, old rose and pale pink – soft colours that convey an evocative glamour. But as this is not an essay in nostalgia, there is of course a *coup de grâce* – tall turquoise glass candelabra and gilded, frosted glasses – the last a little oriental, and unusual in this setting.

Reem likes this way of combining charm with drama, and her look is about texture – an element that is frequently forgotten when it comes to setting a table. For example, she uses a variety of different finishes of glass – mirrored, sandblasted, frosted, engraved, embossed and gilded – and considers that all these various textures not only can, but actually should, be used together.

Above
A mosaic mirror-topped table is set with wavy-edged square plates from Lenox, decorative plates hand-made in the Lebanon, tall, cranberry-stemmed wine glasses and opaline gilded tumblers.

Right
A softer setting for the same decorative Lebanese plates set on an old silk shawl with opaline tumblers and ornate, highly decorated wine jugs.

Opposite
Here, Reem starts with unusual shots of colour from her textiles, which include fuchsia and turquoise upholstered antique chairs and a 200-year old shot-silk cloth from Uzbekistan. This exotic cloth forms a background for a setting of Lenox plates, antique silver candle holders, and extremely contemporary Japanese wine glasses with asymmetrical rims, from Hoia.

Peri Wolfman

Peri Wolfman's style – as befits the Vice President of Product Development for US-based china company Williams-Sonoma – is as up-to-date as it gets, but without any element of shock tactics; it does not grab you nor shout for attention. Instead, it is understated, subtle, simple and extremely sophisticated. In the New England farmhouse she shares with her husband, photographer Charles Gold, and their children, the tones are soft and calm; there are no added shots of bright, vivid accent colours, nor startling, head-turning contrasts. Her look is half old world, half new, the colours are 18th-century early American country colour, and much of the furniture is antique, painted and simple.

The tables Peri lays are as informal and relaxed as the rest of the interior decoration, and it is evident that good food and cheerful eating are as important as the decoration. Peri and Charlie's plates, bowls and platters tend to be big, bold and white, as white works with any and every type of food. Their basic dinner plates are large (buffet size) and look wonderful on their own or with other tableware on top. Their glasses are, on the whole, fairly traditional in style.

Above
Peri is reproducing, together with Spode, some original transferware for Williams-Sonoma, using her own collection and Spode's extensive archives. The oak leaf border plates are one such design, chosen because they can easily be combined with plain modern china.

Left and opposite
Peri and Charlie prove that a table does not have to be elaborate to be interesting. Plain white china, some English ironstone, some by Apilco, is used with classically shaped glasses and traditional cutlery. There is very little table decoration, save for the two large pumpkins – one is real, the other a traditional covered ceramic tureen. The table is completed by the extra-large napkins hung over the back of each chair – a welcoming gesture to the guests.

Nathalie Hambro

Nathalie Hambro is many things – a writer, a cook and a designer of jewellery, handbags and other accessories, and now clothes with her new brand, 'Secours Populaire'. So it is not surprising that she has decided, and original, views on what makes a good contemporary table. She does not think in terms of old or new, and likes to combine objects of all ages: 'What I like now is the way you can mix and match, which also means that when you buy antique china or glass, you can buy odd numbers – it doesn't matter. The point is to take interesting objects and blur the divide, put them together and see how they work together on a table; if it feels right and I like them, then that's it.'

For Nathalie, the starting point for the table is the food: 'I love food, and I think it's very important that it looks seductive on the table; even if I eat on my own, I like to have the right plate and utensils – even if I'm standing up!' It is the sensual aspect of eating and looking at things that is important to her. Each sense has to be satisfied, from sight to taste – wonderful food must not be put on unattractive plates or vice versa. China and glass, she feels, relate to hospitality, to having friends around the table, and the way that they are used contributes greatly to the pleasure of the whole experience.

Nathalie's collection of textiles, which range from antique kimonos to old saris and pieces of embroidery, are frequently used as tablecloths. She explains, 'These days I rarely use a tablecloth – or at any rate, something designed specifically as a tablecloth. If I do put something on the table it is to be part of the story; if I am using Japanese-inspired china, for example, I might spread an antique kimono, or a piece of some other textile that echoes the colour on the table. Not very practical, I know, but I'm not much into "practical" – life is too short.'

Opposite and left
In her London kitchen, Nathalie uses china, glass, colour and texture with abandon and brio. Coloured glass is everywhere – on open shelves, on the table and forged into the pendant lamp. On the kitchen table she has used a beautiful lilac piece of embroidery, on which is set a profusion of purples and greens – cranberry and green drinking glasses, old night-light and candle holders, English green majolica and fat coloured-glass carafes. The food is a mixture of green and white, and the whole effect is both lively and welcoming.

using china & glass around the house

People who are passionate collectors of china and glass are not content with just using their beautiful pieces at the table – they want to look at them all the time. To this end, they may choose to put the objects on display (see pp.148–67) or use them in new and imaginative ways, and for purposes other than those for which they were designed. China and glass are so adaptable, and it is fascinating to see how many uses people can find for their pieces, not only at the table but all around the house.

Opposite
An attractive 19th-century moulded relief jug filled with pretty garden flowers combines beauty and simplicity with practicality.

China and glass are both easily commandeered for use in parts of the house other than the kitchen and dining room. Ceramic bowls are called into play to hold everything from cotton wool to cotton reels. They look attractive with potted plants or flowering bulbs, and instead of practical plastic containers, many people collect small china bowls to store left-overs – they somehow immediately make the food look more appetising.

Old-fashioned ginger jars, often found without their lids, double as a vase for roses or other flowers that will tumble over the sides; old tobacco jars are the ideal height for pens and pencils; and soup tureens are among the most useful of containers – they are ideal for storing keys, dog leads and other important hall necessities, and also make good pots for plants and bulbs. Even the humble china or earthenware toast rack, once found on every breakfast table, is good to hold postcards and other stationery. Pickle dishes – those little flat, sometimes slightly curved dishes, which were widely made in the 18th and 19th centuries – can be scattered liberally everywhere and may generally be used for holding everything from cigarette ash to soap, and hairgrips to cheese straws. A spill holder, which once contained wooden tapers used for lighting candles and pipes, was last spotted in a bathroom used as a cotton bud holder – a definite improvement on the see-through plastic tub.

Many people buy old teacups when they see them; the variety of patterns and designs made during the 18th and 19th centuries mean that they can be widely found at relatively low cost.

Opposite (top left)
Imaginative thought gives many solutions. Here, a tray is used to hold lemons and a small jelly mould makes a perfect salt cellar.

Opposite (top right)
Glass shapes, pretty enough in themselves, are even prettier when grouped together; a measuring jug and a jam pot are holders for a collection of glass stirrers, spoons, sugar crushers and pickle forks.

Opposite (bottom right)
Old-fashioned mixing bowls and moulds are good for storage too, preferably where their comfortable shapes may be appreciated.

Right
A collection of china, all of it functional, has been grouped together and displayed in a decorative and original way.

Below
A glass jar holds a collection of china sugar crushers and spoons.

Although originally designed for tea, these cups are just as pretty used for coffee at the end of a meal.

Jugs in all their shapes and sizes are the loveliest of containers for flowers, particularly simple bunches of spring or garden flowers (see p.141); jugs can also hold wooden spoons in the kitchen, or toothbrushes in the bathroom, in fact anything that comes in untidy quantities; William Yeoward (see pp.120–21) uses a large pitcher to store lavatory rolls.

Glass is, in many ways, even more adaptable than china. As Trish Foley, US-based Irish designer, writer, and china and glass collector, says: 'Glass is so adaptable – I use drinking glasses not only for drink, but also for sorbets, condiments, and even to hold teaspoons. Most puddings look prettier in a wine glass.' And coloured glass looks even more attractive than clear glass – tumblers of different shades can be used for knives, forks and spoons. Trish uses old French jam and jelly jars for storing teaspoons (see p.146) as they are so much easier to get at than when they are lost in the back of a drawer. She also uses decanters for almost everything: 'Whenever a liquid is on display – decant it; somewhere there

Kate Dyson (see pp.126–27)

Below

A trio of narrow ceramic pitchers is placed at the back of a buffet table as a foil to the setting in front. When using three of a kind, the finished effect is considerably more striking if only one species is used in all three containers. The flowers are, of course, chosen to team with the lilac and white transfer-printed plates.

Opposite

Kate Dyson (see pp.126–27) has been collecting these miniature blue and white jugs since she was a child. She uses them here, balanced on a glass compote dish, as the smallest of flower holders, each one crammed with a tiny bunch of flowers from the garden. They add the final touch to the blue and white table.

Left
Compote dishes were originally designed to be displayed during the dessert course, holding either puddings or elaborate displays of fruit. Today, the dessert table is usually simpler, but the charming shapes of these dishes still look pretty filled with fruit and sweets on a table, either used singly, or in pyramid fashion, a smaller dish balanced within a larger one.

Below
An old glass jelly or jam jar is an excellent container for teaspoons, allowing them to be seen and retrieved at will.

is the perfect decanter. Oils for cooking, bath oil, washing-up liquid and liquid soap, even juices at the table, look much more appetising in pretty, old bottles or decanters [see pp.88–91] than in their shop containers.'

Glass jars and tumblers can be used on the desk for pens and pencils, particularly when they are engraved or gilded. When glass is used for storing something else made of glass – as antique dealer and designer Daniel Rozensztroch does with his glass sugar crushers kept in an old glass measuring jug (see p.142) – it makes an interesting picture in itself.

Drinking glasses are perfect for holding flowers – small goblets for violets or primroses and straight-sided glasses for long-stemmed blooms. Even celery glasses – those 19th-century, stemmed, tall goblets, often of moulded or pressed glass – are ideal for a bunch of flowers to be displayed on a small table, their comparative height and narrow base lending themselves to decorative floral arrangements. Coloured glasses can be used even more effectively for a striking composition – for example, a dark purple glass with deep red roses, a bright green glass with daffodils, or a Bristol blue tumbler with white daisies.

Above
The more delicate antique compote dishes – some of which were made to very high standards – are often better used ornamentally as part of a display because they can be highly fragile.

Top right
A 19th-century deep glass syllabub or trifle bowl finds a different use as an attractive pot-pourri holder.

Right
This pineapple holder, dating from the late 18th century, is here being used as its maker originally intended, but these intriguing objects may also be used as long-stemmed flower vases.

display & storage

Left

It is an art to transform ordinary, everyday objects into an immediately interesting display. In Glen Senk and Keith Johnson's Philadelphia kitchen, a variety of small, decorative coffee/cereal bowls have become instant decoration by simply stacking them upside down. Not only are they something to look at in the whole, but each pattern can now be appreciated for its own sake.

Opposite

The Senk/Johnson kitchen (see also pp.160–61) is notable for the way in which everything in it is displayed and juxtaposed. In addition to bowls stacked upside down, there is another set stacked base to base, almost like ceramic dumbbells. Four faience plates are hung down the bookshelves. Indeed, the whole room is a celebration of ceramic art.

Display and storage of china and glass are, in many ways, inextricably entwined. Both the decorative and the functional have to have a home, and in some cases it is merely a question of composition and arrangement that divide the two. Glen Senk and Keith Johnson, for example, of the successful Anthropologie stores, which sell innovative, must-have household objects from all over the world, collect old and new china and glass and have it all over the house; they believe in making an attractive display out of the stored china, and the pieces are in frequent use.

Senk and Johnson have few rules where display is concerned. Shape and pattern are the deciding factors when choosing pieces for display, and they feel that new china and glass, if mixed with older pieces, work best if they are simple in form.

Displayed on open shelves is a collection of naïve lustreware bowls (see above), each one pretty in itself but even more effective as a group; instead of stacking them inside each other, they up-end them and build an acrobat's tower, where each pattern can be seen; in another variation, they take two colours of the same shape of bowl, and on one shelf show a group of blue, on another a group predominately red. Along the same wall, Quimper faience plates have been hung in a line on the uprights of a bookcase (see opposite) – it is the unusual juxtaposition that attracts the eye. This surprise to the eye is one of the first essentials to good decorating, and these principles apply as much to the miniature as to the large – so mix the practical and useful with the odd and the beautiful, and keep in mind the principles of scale and harmony.

Opposite
An 18th-century faux-bamboo painted cabinet protects and displays creamware dating from the same period.

Left
Another collection of 18th-century creamware set on freestanding shelves, which display to best advantage the delicately pierced and moulded dishes.

Below
Quimper pottery, old and new, is displayed in a white-painted cabinet; the cheerful, sometimes naïve colours and designs of the Quimper are set off against the plainness of the cupboard.

Ann Mollo, film and garden designer, has a large, fine collection of antique English creamware that is displayed simply and beautifully (see opposite and left), for she knows that the better it is displayed, the more attractive it looks. She keeps much of her collection in an antique faux-bamboo cupboard (see opposite), where she arranges a small tableau, carefully choosing the pieces so that each shape is viewed at its best and something of the history of the genre can be seen and understood. She also keeps some pieces in a pretty corner cupboard – a good home for them since the depth of the shelf gives enough room for a composition with more than one dimension.

Previous pages (p.152)
Dressers were one of the first pieces of furniture to be built with a specific purpose – to both store and display household dishes. This painted Irish dresser is home to a collection of blue and white 19th-century Spode as well as miscellaneous blue and white items, a set of antique wine-glass coolers, and assorted silver salts.

Previous pages (p.153)
This dresser, belonging to Kate Dyson (see pp.126–27), is a testament to the power of storage as display. The base was bought in a sale, and the shelves were built around it. Although crammed with what at first seems a haphazard arrangement of glass and china, it soon becomes clear that every piece has been carefully chosen to make an interesting overall picture.

Quimper faience (see previous page) is naïve and charming; it would be overwhelmed were it displayed in grand surroundings, so Victoria du Roure (see pp.128–29), who loves the charm of this French pottery and has a small, fascinating collection of antique designs, displays it in a country cupboard of simple lines that complements the pottery on its shelves.

Peri Wolfman (see pp.136–37) displays her collection of transfer-print plates on shelving above wide, built-in, painted dressers either side of the door in her living room; linking the two sets of shelves is a narrow shelf over the door filled with white china pitchers. Below and among the plates, which are carefully arranged according to colour and pattern, are other pieces of her collection of white and cream ceramics, each piece selected for its design qualities, as well as its more practical merits: a set of cups and saucers are stacked in two rows, each handle carefully aligned to the right; bowls stack up next to dishes and plates. The whole wall is interesting to look at, for this is display at its simplest and most effective.

Above
A very Swedish arrangement, with everything chosen and placed so that there is space between every element. By the traditional stove, a wall-hung plate rack holds part of a typically Swedish blue and white service, while other pieces are displayed on the buffet beneath.

Left
Although this arrangement is primarily functional, there is a pleasing air to it – something to do with the way that the objects have been placed with care rather than stored willy-nilly. Each piece has been given its own space, and enough of it, making sure that everything is not only easily at hand, but also seen at its best.

Opposite
Display at its simple best. Peri Wolfman stores and displays as much as possible on open shelves so that she can enjoy her collection. Here, her transfer-printed plates and functional china are linked by an overdoor shelf of white pitchers that draws the two sides of the room together.

Opposite

New York-based interior decorator Anthony Cochrane has conceived an attractive and practical display of white china. Plates of differing sizes, shapes and designs are grouped in a pleasing way, each shape balanced and counter-balanced. The secret with wall-hung displays is to work out first, on a flat surface, which shapes and colours work best next to each other by moving them around until the whole is visually satisfying.

Below

Large serving plates form an attractive display in themselves, but they also transform the surrounding objects – the narrow mirror, twin table lamps and chest of drawers – into a strong and coherent composition.

Right

These apparently disparate objects – a wooden paddle, metal jelly and blancmange moulds, a sconce and two antique blue and white plates – create an intriguing and amusing culinary display on a kitchen wall.

Bottom right

A dark, heavy, wall-hung display stand has been brightened and lightened by being used as the centrepiece for a display of attractive ceramics; even the metal towel rail below is drawn into the arrangement.

Large, striking pieces look good on their own or grouped with other objects where their lines can be easily seen and appreciated. William Yeoward (see pp.120–21) likes to show impressive ceramic pieces, such as a swooping curved antique tureen, in solitary splendour on a shelf, a mantel, or an item of furniture. Glen Senk and Keith Johnson (see pp.150–51) have a similar approach: on a window sill in their Philadelphia kitchen, a composition of tall glass canisters and cream ceramic containers are a real pleasure to see, backed by the verdant landscape outside (see right). On the mantel above a range (see opposite), a carefully composed group of serving dishes, platters and pretty objects are there to be used as well as admired, and on a marble slab some examples of early American pottery are displayed but also used to hold vegetables – and a few alabaster eggs. Hanging on the wall is a seemingly naïve but actually carefully considered arrangement, consisting of miscellaneous kitchen accessories (see previous page).

Opposite (top right and below left)
Jugs, storage jars, and other pieces of kitchen paraphernalia are displayed for their looks and contrasting textures.

Opposite (bottom left)
Tureens are beautiful objects and should never be stored away. They look best placed where their bulbous shapes can be enjoyed.

Below
The deep mantelpiece above the range acts as a convenient storage shelf and a striking display area.

By its very nature, glass seems as if its natural state is to be on display and admired; from the first Roman cameo glass vases to ornamented Venetian fantasies to 18th- and 19th-century wonders of cut, etched and engraved glass, it was always meant to be regarded for its beauty as well as used for a practical purpose.

Many people do just that, keeping their glassware out for all to see and enjoy. Nathalie Hambro (see pp.138–39), a self-confessed glass admirer who collects a wide range of glass including coloured and heavily textured kinds, likes to put pieces out, on the dining table for instance, where she will play with colour, combining green with mauve glass, or black with red. She also creates interesting displays by placing a variety of different clear glass objects together on a metal surface so that the hard metal reflects back the light of the glass.

New York fashion designer Reem Acra (see pp.134–35) is also intrigued by glass, and recently began to collect antique glassware – heavy, antique tumblers and goblets, coloured, decorated, gilded and ornamented with engravings; she uses them on the table in conjunction

Opposite
Glass arranged attractively on a butler's tray includes decanters, carafes, cocktail glasses and jugs.

Above
Collectors of glass are always taken by the variety of shapes available. Glass almost always looks best displayed en masse, where each shape flatters that of its neighbour.

Right
The common denominator here is bulk – each of these pieces veers towards the large, and therefore the objects look best grouped together to keep them in scale.

Overleaf (p.164)
An antique tiered-glass sweetmeats dish holds multi-coloured chocolate beans, presenting a colourful and appetising display.

Overleaf (p.165)
Nathalie Hambro has created a highly original and artistically inspired lampshade made from a collection of old glasses.

Above
Paris-based antique dealer and
designer Daniel Rozensztroch has
chosen to display green-tinted
glass together on a polished black
surface and anchored by an
unusual, sculpture-like fantasy
light; the effect is both striking
and effective.

Left
An old stove is used as part
cupboard, part display case for
a collection of interesting shapes
in clear glass. The white-painted
brick wall behind sets off the
unusual decorative glass vessels
on top of the stove.

with her collection of modern glass, and when they are not in use they stand in a carefully selected space against a background of rich turquoise, which shows them off to great effect.

Moussie Sayers, Swedish interior designer and owner of the Nordic Style shop in London, collects and displays an unusual collection of delicate, silver-lidded claret jugs on a tray in her dining room (see below). No two jugs are the same, and each one was designed as an individual wine holder to sit in front of every place setting. Decanters were also designed to be looked at as well as used, and many glass collectors like to display them in a room where the variety of design and line can be appreciated (see pp.90–91). Like so many pieces of glass, they look better massed together – Daniel Rozensztroch (see opposite) groups his decanters together on a tray. Actually, he enjoys displaying much of his

glass in carefully arranged groups. A small collection of once-utilitarian pale green glass – everything from custard pots to cake stands – is massed together on a black iron chest, and a wood-burning iron stove is used as a display case for clear glass, some kept on the top, and other pieces stored where the fire once burned.

Below
Old claret jugs are things of beauty in themselves. They are even more beautiful when displayed together en masse, like a flock of birds about to take flight, so that the diversity of shape and pattern can really be appreciated.

storage & care

The pleasure of collecting china and glass is for all to see; the less desirable aspect is that both are extremely fragile: pieces can crack, chip and shatter, and it is sadness itself to see a treasured object broken into smithereens. However, a combination of carefully considered storage, coupled with taking a few practical steps to eliminate possible damage, can prolong the life of any piece, while still giving maximum visual satisfaction.

Opposite
There is no reason why storage should be dull and uninspiring; for those who love their china and glass, the manner in which it is all put away can give just as much pleasure as the way it is displayed in more formal surroundings.

Opposite and below
Swedish interior designer Moussie Sayers, owner of the Nordic Style shop in London, stores her china in the most subtle and witty way. She has various open shelf systems for china storage; some are backed with tiles that have had motifs from the china patterns painted directly onto them; elsewhere, the wooden shelves and the surrounds are decorated.

storing china

This page and opposite
A china cupboard does not need to be conventional and obvious – with a little lateral thinking, many unusual and interesting storage solutions can be found. This early 20th-century metal cupboard, owned by antique dealer and designer Daniel Rozensztroch, started life in an industrial context but nevertheless works extremely well in a smart Paris living room. The cupboard houses both everyday ware and antique decorative ceramics, such as a collection of old spongeware bowls. It has the practical advantage of not being too deep, thereby making it simple to retrieve particular pieces.

Since we tend to use china every day of our lives, we inevitably come to cherish particular pieces, so it is well worth taking care to ensure their continuing survival. Such care pays, as is evidenced by the large quantity of old china still in existence today. But it is not just antique china that should be well looked after; new ceramics – the collectable china of both now and the future – should be equally cared for.

China that is hand-painted or has any sort of surface decoration, such as gilding or beading, as well as old china, should be washed by hand. The water in a modern dishwasher is simply too hot and the dishwasher detergent far too harsh for delicate ceramics. In the 19th century, large houses had wooden washing basins specifically to wash fragile china and glass, the average porcelain sink being liable to crack them. Today, wooden sinks are rarely an option, but old china should still be washed with care; many suggest a plastic bowl inside a porcelain or stainless steel sink, and as a counsel of true perfection, a folded towel could be folded in the bottom of

chargers accrued by its wealthy owner. Cupboards were originally made to be carried around as the owner moved from dwelling to dwelling; over time – as with all other pieces of domestic furniture – the cupboard became more sophisticated and less portable.

Of course, china that you use on a regular basis does not have to be stored in a cupboard. Many would say that it looks better massed together on a shelf or dresser, in a buffet, under a sideboard or even on the table. The humble plate rack – once a necessity above the kitchen sink, now sometimes redundant due to the ubiquity of the dishwasher – is an ideal permanent storage area for plates: not only is it an attractive and practical way of draining dishes, but china is more accessible than when it is stored in a cupboard. The usefulness of the plate rack can be extended with the addition of a shelf above the rack for bowls and jugs.

It is very much a personal preference whether you favour open or closed storage. Open storage, such as a set of shelves, offers the opportunity to display attractive china as well as providing easier access to frequently used items, yet objects can become dusty or greasy (particularly in a kitchen) and will need more cleaning than those stored in a cupboard.

the bowl. Warm water rather than hot water should be used, and the pieces should, of course, be carefully dried.

Strictly speaking, china should be stored somewhere that is neither too hot nor too cold, because extremes of temperature will weaken the material. When you store hand-painted or gilded china, remember that if you stack plates or bowls, cloth or paper should be put between each piece for protection – a paper napkin will do the trick. Available now are round metal plate racks, slightly reminiscent of old-fashioned tiered cake pedestals, on which plates can be stacked without touching each other. Delicate cups should not be hung from hooks as the handle is the weakest part.

By the 18th century, cupboards – or dressers, which are really open cupboards – were being built in most large houses in Europe. A cupboard, as its name suggests, was originally a board, or set of boards (early shelves in fact; the doors were added later), designed to show off the silver-plated cups, bowls and

Opposite
This great collection of bowls, dishes and containers, stored beneath the old French farmhouse table in Peri Wolfman's country kitchen in Bridgehampton, New York, means that they are close at hand for cooking. Although they are simply arranged, there is an order and a precision involving corresponding shapes and sizes being carefully stacked together.

Above
Glass-fronted cupboards offer the perfect combination of displaying a collection of china while protecting the pieces from dust and grease.

A good compromise might be glass cupboard doors (see p.175); these
are either clear (so that the china is both fully visible and protected),
frosted, or in an etched or blasted design. Even if you are storing china
behind solid closed doors, always arrange it as if it were on display – that
is, edit and define what you have, arranging it either by colour, material,
shape or pattern, and keep it as tidy as possible so it is easier to find the
right piece for the job.

Now that the kitchen, and its design, plays such an important part in our
lives, designers are spending much time and thought devising interesting
and practical forms of storage for food and kitchen equipment, and many
of their good ideas can be borrowed for china storage. For example, the
principle of the wide, deep saucepan drawer, which pulls out at the gentle
touch of the hand, can be adapted for large pieces of china. Metal basket
shelves, with high sides that slide out from a cupboard and originally
designed to hold tins and jars, can be used for plates, jugs, cups, mugs
and small bowls. Many utensil and small equipment drawers have divisions
within them so that items can be stored separately and safely; this idea
works just as well with small pieces of ceramic or glass.

storing glass

By its very nature, glass is fragile, and the thinner it is the more delicate it tends to be. Ideally, old glass – and many people would say all new glass, too – should never be washed in a dishwasher. Whether or not you succumb to washing new glass automatically, it is essential that any cut, etched, gilded or coloured pieces must join the hand-washing queue. Glass is easily scratched – particularly lead crystal – so wash glass items in a plastic bowl with a mild detergent and take off any rings before handling the pieces, because the metal and stones can easily mark the surface. Rinse in warm water and dry with a lint-free cloth.

When you store drinking glasses, place them upright, for the rim is the weakest part and can easily chip on a shelf; make sure that any stoppers in decanters or jugs are not too firmly embedded, as two pieces of glass under pressure will cement together – something that can also happen when too many glasses are stacked together in a pile.

When it comes to glass, storage and display are often one and the same thing. Lovers of

Opposite
These practical metal open shelves perfectly complement this functional collection of moulded, pressed and plain glass.

Above
Experts say that glasses should be kept upright so that the bowl – the most fragile part – does not chip. This is especially true of antique glasses, which, although they can be reground to remove chips, are usually weakened by the process.

Left
Not text book storage perhaps, but when these simple, low-stemmed flutes are arranged in this manner they become as much sculpture as storage.

Opposite
Trish Foley, Irish writer and stylist, keeps her glass arranged en masse in a tall built-in cupboard, where the shelves are covered with white self-adhesive plastic cloth. Instead of being cut to size, the cloth flaps over the edge of the shelf a little, resembling a starched white linen runner or heavy, new paper.

Below
True to her view that glass and china are best kept on view and on hand, Peri Wolfman (see pp.136–37) ranges her glasses on accessible open shelves. The tumblers line the top shelf, while below wine glasses are slotted into specially made brackets, so they can be stored safely and extracted easily.

Opposite
Paris-based designer and antique dealer Daniel Rozensztroch stores his antique coloured glass in an unusual metal cupboard. Many of the pieces are moulded or pressed, ranging from pale green to deep amber. The glasses, of different colours and textures, are both stored and displayed, the dark recesses of the cupboard making them glow like jewels.

Left
Nathalie Hambro (see pp.138–39) has a way with glass that may seem simple, but which is in fact carefully thought out: pieces are stacked with seeming haphazardness, and she makes sure that there is a certain confusion in the final mix, which adds richness and interest.

Below
Milky opaline glass, so simple and so perfect, is stored and shown off in an old bottle holder, the black wire contrasting with the soft white glass.

glass like to see their pieces, so they tend to store them where they are easily accessible and where they can be viewed to best effect.

Glass appears to alter in colour and texture depending on the surface on which it is displayed; glass on a glass shelf, for example, can take on an almost ethereal quality, particularly when the background colour is deep enough to highlight the design. Glass on metal seems harder and sharper, while glass on a fabric- or paper-covered shelf looks much softer. Choose a surface that is in harmony with other elements of the decorative scheme.

Sophisticated effects can be achieved with the careful use of lighting: glass that is lit from beneath a glass shelf or table is one way of showing off the material in an artistic way, especially when the pieces are cut or otherwise decorated. The other option is to use lighting as you would for a picture or sculpture, with directional spotlights that highlight the shape and the decorative qualities of the objects.

china & glass directory

Specialist china suppliers

Baltic Trader
(Polish stoneware)
The Old Needlemakers
West Street
Lewes
East Sussex BN7 2NZ
T: 01273 483449
F: 01273 478419
www.baltictrader.co.uk
E: info@baltictrader.co.uk

Belleek Pottery
(Fine Parian china)
T: 00 28 6865 9314
F: 00 28 6865 8625
www.belleek.com
E: customerservices@belleek.ie

Bridgewater Pottery Ltd.
739 Fulham Road
London SW6 5UL
T: 020 7371 9077
F: 020 7384 2457
Email: mailorder@bwpottery.co.uk

Chinacraft Ltd
Parke House
130 Barlby Road
London W10 6BW
T: 020 7565 5876
www.chinacraft.co.uk
E: info@chinacraft.co.uk

China Etc Ltd
21 Shepperton Road
Staines, Middlesex TW18 1SE
T: 01784 491604
F: 01784 454411

Collection REGARDS
(Astier de Villatte)
2, rue de L'Olive
37 500 Chinon
France
T: 0033 2 47 93 34 24

F: 0033 2 47 93 00 11
www.collection-regards.com
E: infos@collection-regards.com

Country Traditionals
(Eunzlau ceramics – Polish stoneware)
15 St Christopher's Place
London W1M 5HD
T: 020 7486 1101
www.countrytraditionals.com

David Mellor
4 Sloane Square
London SW1 8EE
T: 020 7730 4259

The Denby Pottery Co.
Denby
Derbyshire DE5 8NX
T: 01773 740899
F: 01773 570211
E: consumer.services@denby.co.uk

Dibor
(French shapes in ceramic and glass)
20a West Park
Harrogate
North Yorkshire HG1 1BJ
T: 0870 0133 666
www.dibor.co.uk

Essentially White Ltd
(china, featuring much of the Pillivuyt
all-white range – everything from eggcups
to cake stands)
T: 01732 521 558.
www.essentiallywhite.co.uk
E: info@essentiallywhite.co.uk

James Sadler
13 Boon Hill
Bignall End
Stoke-on-Trent
Staffordshire ST7 8LA
T: 01782 720754
F: 01782 720754
www.staffordshirechina.com
E: sales @ staffordshirechina.com

La Maison des Lices
(French country faience, china and glass)
2 Boulevard Louis-Blanc
83990 Saint-Tropez
South of France
T: 00 33 04 94 97 64 64
www.la-maison-des-lices.com

OKA Direct Ltd
(Very good tableware, glassware
and pale-glazed china)
Chene Court
Poundwell Street,
Modbury,
Devon PL21 0QJ
T: 0870 160 6002
F 0158 832 001
www.okadirect.com

Poole Pottery Ltd
Sopers Lane
Poole
Dorset BH17 7PP
T: 01202 666200
F: 01202 682894
www.poolepottery.co.uk
E: sales@poolepottery.co.uk

Portmeirion Potteries Ltd
(Manufactures an extensive range of
tableware, bakeware, kitchenware and
giftware)
London Road
Stoke-on-Trent
Staffordshire ST4 7QQ
T: 01782 744721
F: 01782 744061

La Provence Collections Ltd
(A specialist French importer of table linens,
glassware and ceramics)
T: 01451 870317 for wedding list service
www.laprovence.co.uk

Reject China Shop
183 Brompton Road
London, SW3 1NF
T: 020 7581 0739

Royal Creamware Fine China
Royal Chintz
World Wide Shopping Mall Ltd
Chancery Lane
Malton
North Yorkshire YO17 7HW
T: 01653 602 880
F: 01653 602 889
www.royal-creamware.co.uk

Royal Crown Derby
(Porcelain and bone china)
194 Osmaston Road
Derby DE23 8JZ
T: 01332 712800
F: 01332 712863
www.royal-crown-derby-co.uk
E: enquiries@royal-crown-derby.co.uk

Royal Doulton plc,
Sir Henry Doulton House
Forge Lane
Etruria
Stoke-on-Trent
Staffordshire ST1 5NN
T: 01782 404045
F: 01782 404254
www.royal-doulton.com

Royal Winton
Normacot Road
Longton
Stoke-on-Trent
Staffordshire ST3 1PA
T: 01782 598811
F: 01782 342737
www.royalwinton.co.uk
E: info@royalwinton.co.uk

Royal Worcester
Severn Street
Worcester WR1 2NE
T: 01905 23221
F: 01905 23601
E: rwgeneral@royal-worcester.co.uk

Small Island Trader Ltd
(China and crystal specialist)
Brockton Hall
Brockton
Staffordshire ST21 6LY
T: 01785 851 800
F: 01785 851 900

Spode
Church Street
Stoke-on-Trent
Staffordshire ST4 1BX
T: 01782 744011
F: 01782 744220
www.spode.co.uk
E: spode@spode.co.uk

The Wedgwood Visitor Centre
(Designers include Jasper Conran, Kelly
Hoppen and Paul Costelloe)
Barlaston
Stoke-on-Trent
Staffordshire ST12 9ES
T: 01782 282986
F: 01782 374083
www.wedgwood.com
E: customer.care@wedgwood.com

Thomas Goode & Co
(Renowned as one of the best bone china,
crystal and silverware shop in the world)
19 South Audley Street
London W1K 2BN
T: 020 7499 2823
F: 020 7629 4230
www.thomasgoode.com
E: info@thomasgoode.co.uk

Villeroy & Boch (UK) Ltd
267 Merton Road
London SW18 5JS
T: 020 8871 0011

Specialist glass suppliers

Dartington Crystal
Linden Close
Torrington
Devon EX38 7AN
T: 01805 626424
F: 01805 626263
www.dartington.co.uk

The Glass Shop
424 Edgware Road
London, W2 1EG
T: 020 7706 1099

Rossella Junck Gallery
(Specialists in 19th and 20th century
Murano glass and contemporary glass)
San Marco 2360
Calle delle Ostreghe
30124 Venice
Italy
T: 00 39 0 41 520 77 47

Nina Campbell
(Handblown venetian glassware and
cranberry glass)
9 Walton Street
London SW3 2JD
T: 0207 225 1011
F: 0207 225 0644
info@ninacampbell.com

Robert Welch Designs
(Contemporary classical glass)
Lower High St
Chipping Camden
Gloucestershire GL55 6DY
T: 01386 840 522
www.robertwelch.com

Salviati
(Specialists in Venetian glass)
Fondamenta RADI 16
I-30141 Murano
Venice
Italy
T: 00 33 0 321 95 96 22
F: 00 33 0 321 12 79 26
www.salviati.com

Vessel
114 Kensington Park Road
London W11
T: 020 7727 8001

Waterford Crystal Visitor Centre
Kilbarry, Waterford
Ireland
T: 00353 51 332500
F: 00353 51 332716
www.waterfordcrystalvisitorcentre.com
William Yeoward Crystal
336 King's Road
London SW3 5UR
www.williamyeowardcrystal.com
E: office@williamyeowardcrystal.co.uk

Department stores and stockists of china and glass

Alessi (UK) Ltd.
22 Brook Street
London W1K 5DF
T: 020 75189090
F: 020 75189080

Aria
295-7 Upper Street
London N1 2TU
T: 020 7704 1999
T: 020 7704 6333
www.aria-shop.co.uk
E: design@ariashop.co.uk

The Conran Shop
Michelin House
81 Fulham Road
London SW3
T: 020 7589 7401
www.conran.co.uk

Churchill "Choices" range
(Linda Barker collection)
www.churchill-direct.com

Divertimenti
33-34 Marylebone High Street
London W1U 4PT
T: 020 7935 0689
www.divertimenti.co.uk

General Trading Company Ltd
2 Symons Street
London SW3 2TJ
Tel: 020 7730 0411
www.general-trading.co.uk

Harrods
87-135 Brompton Road
London SW1X 7XL
T: 020 7730 1234
www.harrods.com

Habitat
196 Tottenham Court Road
London W1P 9LD
T: 0845 601 0740 for branches
www.habitat.co.uk

Harvey Nichols
109-125 Knightsbridge
London SW1X 7RJ
T: 020 7235 5000
www.harveynichols.com

Heal's
196 Tottenham Court Road
London W1P 9LD
T: 020 7636 1666
www.heals.com

IKEA UK
Head Office
IKEA Brent Park
2 Drury Lane
North Circular Road
London NW10 0TH
T: 020 8208 5600
www.ikea.com

John Lewis
278-306 Oxford Street
London W1E 5NN
T: 020 7828 1000 for details of branches
www.johnlewis.com

Kelly Hoppen shop
175-177 Fulham Road
London SW3 6JW
Tel: 020 7351 1910
www.kellyhoppen.com

Liberty
210-220 Regent Street
London
T: 020 7734 1234
www.liberty.co.uk

La Marrakech
64 Goldborne Road
London W10 5PS
T: 020 8964 8307

Muji
187 Oxford Street
London W1
T: 020 7437 7503
T: 020 7323 2208 for details of branches

Nordic Style
109 Lots Road
London
SW10 0RN
T: 0 207 351 1755
F: 0 207 351 4966
E: sales@nordicstyle.com

Purves & Purves
80-81 & 83 Tottenham Court Road
London W1
T: 020 7580 8223
www.purves.co.uk

Selfridges & Co
400 Oxford Street
London W1A 1AB
T: 0870 8377 377
F: 020 7495 8321
www.selfridges.com
contactservices@selfridges.co.uk

Auction houses and fairs

Christies
(Auction house for specialist one-off pieces)
85 Old Brompton Road
London SW7 3LD
T: 020 7930 6074
www.christies.com

Sotheby's
(Decorative art and design pieces)
34-35 New Bond Street
London W1A 2AA
Tel: 020 7293 5000
www.sothebys.com

Bonhams
65-69 Lots Road
London SW10
Tel: 020 7393 3900

National Glass Collectors Fair (UK)
www.glassfairs.co.uk

China matching and search services

Tablewhere?
(Discontinued china matching service)
4 Queen's Parade Close
London N11 3FY
T: 020 8361 6111
www.tablewhere.co.uk

China Search
(Many discontinued patterns of English china)
PO Box 1202
Kenilworth
Warwickshire CV8 2WW
www.chinasearch.co.uk

Antique shops, markets and factory outlets

Alfie's Antiques Market
13-25 Church Street
London NW8 8DT
T: 020 7723 6066

Camden Passage
(An array of antique china and glass stalls)
Upper Street
Islington
London, N1

Claudio Bezoari
(Anique glass, including Bohemian French including St. Louis, Baccarat, Opaline)
Unit 5 Crown Arcade
119 Portobello Road
London W11
T: 020 7792 3619
E-mail: elmauk@nw2000.co.uk

Jeanette Hayhurst
(Antique glass specialist)
32A Kensington Church Street
London W8 4HA
T: 0207 938 1539

Josphine Ryan Antiques and Interiors
63 Abbeville Road
London SW4 9JW
T: 0208 675 3900
www.josephineryanantiques.co.uk

Lovers of Blue and White
(Blue and white china both new and antique dating from 1780 to present day)
T: 01763 853 800
www.blueandwhite.com

Portobello China & Woollens Limited:
(Factory outlet for leading British tableware and gifts including: Wedgwood, Royal Doulton, Royal Worcester, Spode, Johnson Brothers, Cornishware. Quality Scottish. Rarely available export designs in stock, also limited editions.)
85 & 89 Portobello Road
London W11 2AB
T: 020 7727 3857
www.portobello-ltd.com
E: info@portobello-ltd.com

David Glick Antique Glass
(18th and 19th century English and Continental glass)
300 Westbourne Grove
London W11
T: 07850 615867

Georgina Jay
(18th and 19th century English, Irish and Scottish decanters, glasses, salts, vases, handcut, blown, etched and engraved)
Crown Arcade
119 Portobello Road
London W11
T: 020 7792 3619
www.georginajayantiques.com

Mallett Antiques
(specialist in 17th, 18th, 19th and 20th century glass, including val Saint-Lambert)
141 New Bond Street
London, W1S 2BS
T: 0 20 7499 7411
F: 0 20 7495 3179
www.malletantiques.com

Manorcroft Antiques:
(A wide range of glass 1840-1940 English and Continental, cranberry, gilded, enamelled, vases, drinking glasses. James Powell, Webbs, Venetian etc. Also Torquay Pottery)
Unit 7, 113 Portobello Road
London W11
T: 07970 747909
www.manorcroft-antiques.com

China and glass repairers

China Repairers
(Repairs domestic ware and antique porcelain and pottery; various levels of restoration.)
The Old Coach House
King St Mews, King Street
London N2 8DY
T: 020 8444 3030.

The Dining Room Shop
(Restores broken pieces and copies to match both china and glass)
62-64 White Hart Lane
London SW13 0PZ
T: 020 8878 1020

Blue Crystal Glass
(They will grind chips from rims and feet of wine glasses and decanters, make new stoppers and make feet for vases or claret jugs, as well as mending other types of glassware. They also supply blue glass liners for silver salt, mustard and sugar holders. 200 stock sizes available)
Units 6-8, 21 Wren Street
London WC1X 0HF
T: 020 7278 0142
www.bluecrystalglass.co.uk

picture credits

Endpapers — a house in the Hamptons designed by Solis Betancourt

I Josephine Ryan's house in London; **2** a house in the Hamptons designed by Solis Betancourt, photograph by Andrew Wood; **3** Ann Mollo's house in London; **4** Anthony Cochrane's apartment in New York; **6** Glen Senk and Keith Johnson's house in Philadelphia; **7** Stephanie Reeves' home in Atlanta, Georgia; **8-9** William Yeoward's house in the country; **10-11** Véronique Lopez's house from Casa Lopez; **13** Ann Mollo's house in London; **14** Josephine Ryan's house in London; **15** above left Home of Pen Wolfman and Charles Gold in Bridgehampton; **15** above right Home Hill Inn in New Hampshire; **15** below Malcome Carefree and Denise Figlar; **16-17** Reem Acra's apartment in New York; **18** Lena Proudlock of Denim In Style's house in Gloucestershire; **19** above Anthony Cochrane's apartment in New York; **19** below Lena Proudlock of Denim In Style's house in Gloucestershire; **20** above Dining room designed by Stephanie Stokes Inc, Interior Design; **20** below Lena Proudlock of Denim In Style's house in Gloucestershire; **21** Kate Dyson of The Dining Room Shop's house in London; **22** above Glen Senk and Keith Johnson's house in Philadelphia; **22** below Stephane & Victoria du Roure's home in New Hampshire; **23** above Glen Senk and Keith Johnson's house in Philadelphia; **23** below Tricia Foley's house on Long Island; **24** Tricia Foley's house on Long Island; **25** above Josephine Ryan's house in London; **25** centre William Yeoward's house in the country; **25** below right Moussie Sayers of Nordic Style's house in London; **26** Tricia Foley's house on Long Island; **27** Ann Mollo's house in London; **28** Home Hill Inn in New Hampshire; **29** above Anthony Cochrane's apartment in New York; **29** below Tricia Foley's house on Long Island; **30** above Daniel Rozensztroch's apartment in Paris; **30** below Moussie Sayers of Nordic Style's house in London; **31** above Tricia Foley's house on Long Island; **31** below left & below right Josephine Ryan's house in London; **32** above Home Hill Inn in New Hampshire; **32** below left & below right William Yeoward's house in the country; **33** Malcome Carefree and Denise Figlar; **34** Tricia Foley's house on Long Island; **35** above & below Dining room designed by Stephanie Stokes Inc, Interior Design; **36** above left Daniel Rozensztroch's apartment in Paris; **36** above right Caroline Clifton-Mogg's house in London: **36** below Anthony Cochrane's apartment in New York; **37** Malcome Carefree and Denise Figlar; **38** Home of Peri Wolfman and Charles Gold in Bridgehampton; **39** above & below Tricia Foley's house on Long Island; **41** Kate Dyson of The Dining Room Shop's house in London; **42** Lena Proudlock of Denim In Style's house in Gloucestershire; **43** Moussie Sayers of Nordic Style's house in London; **44-45** Stephane and Victoria du Roure's house in New Hampshire; **46** Ann Mollo's house in London; **47** above left home of Peri Wolfman and Charles Gold in Bridgehampton; **47** above right Tricia Foley's house on Long Island; **47** bottom right Josephine Ryan's house in London; **48-49** Véronique Lopez's house from Casa Lopez; **49** above Anthony Cochrane's apartment in New York; 49 below Malcome Carefree and Denise Figlar; **50** Lena Proudlock of Denim In Style's house in Gloucestershire; **51** above left above Dining room designed by Stephanie Stokes Inc, Interior Design; SI above right Moussie Sayers of Nordic Style's house in London; SI below Caroline Clifton-Mogg's house in London; **52-53** Caroline Clifton-Mogg's house in London; **54** above Jamie Drake's apartment in New York; **54** below Véronique Lopez's house from Casa Lopez; **55** Jamie Drake's apartment in New York; **57** Dining room designed by Stephanie Stokes Inc., Interior Design; **58** Caroline Clifton-Mogg's house in London; **59** above left Home of Peri Wolfman and Charles Gold in Bridgehampton; **59** above right & below Glen Senk and Keith Johnson's house in Philadelphia; **60** Dining room designed by Stephanie Stokes Inc., Interior Design; **61** Kate Dyson of The Dining Room Shop's house in London; **62** Caroline Clifton-Mogg's house in London; **63** above & below William Yeoward's house in the country; **64-65** Lena Proudlock of Denim In Style's house in Gloucestershire; **66** above left & below Home of Peri Wolfman and Charles Gold in Bridgehampton; **66** below right Daniel Rozensztroch's apartment in Paris; **67** above & below left Dining room designed by Stephanie Stokes Inc. Interior Design; **67** below right Stephanie Reeves' home in Atlanta, Georgia; **68-69** Michael Coorengel and Jean-Pierre Calvagrac's apartment in Paris; **70** above left Glen Senk and Keith Johnson's house in Philadelphia; **70** above right Stephane & Victoria du Roure's home in New Hampshire; **70** below Home Hill Inn in New Hampshire; **71** Stephane & Victoria du Roure's home in New Hampshire; **72** Glen Senk and Keith Johnson's house in Philadelphia; **73** above Daniel Rozensztroch's apartment in Paris; **73** below William Yeoward's house in the country; **74** Caroline Clifton-Mogg's house in London: **75** above Véronique Lopez's house from Casa Lopez; **75** below left & right Kate Dyson of The Dining Room Shop's house in London; **76** William Yeoward's house in the country; **77** Michael Coorengel and Jean-Pierre Calvagrac's apartment in Paris; **78** Nathalie Hambro's house in London; **79** above Nathalie Hambro's house in London; **79** below Véronique Lopez's house from Casa Lopez; **80** above & below William Yeoward's house in the country; **81** above Michael Coorengel and Jean-Pierre Calvagrac's apartment in Paris; **81** below William Yeoward's house in the country; **83** Daniel Rozensztroch's apartment in Paris; **84** Anthony Cochrane's apartment in New York; **85** above Dining room designed by Stephanie Stokes Inc., Interior Design; **85** below left Home Hill Inn in New Hampshire; **85** below right Tricia Foley's house on Long Island; **86** William Yeoward's house in the country; **87** above left William Yeoward's house in the country; **87** above right Caroline Clifton-Mogg's house in London; **87** below Véronique Lopez's house from Casa Lopez; **88** above left & below Josephine Ryan's house in London; **88** above left Tricia Foley's house on Long Island; **89** Tricia Foley's house on Long Island; **90** above & below Michael Coorengel and Jean-Pierre Calvagrac's apartment in Paris; **91** above Michael Coorengel and Jean-Pierre Calvagrac's apartment in Paris; **91** below William Yeoward's house in the country; **92** above Lena Proudlock of Denim In Style's house in Gloucestershire; **92** below William Yeoward's house in the country; **93** below Véronique Lopez's house from Casa Lopez; **94** Kate Dyson of The Dining Room Shop's house in London; **95** Reem Acra's apartment in New York; **96** above Nathalie Hambro's house in London; **96** below Reem Acra's apartment in New York; **97** above Reem Acra's apartment in New York; **97** below Michael Coorengel and Jean-Pierre Calvagrac's apartment in Paris; **98-99** Nathalie Hambro's house in London; **100** above Dominique Lubar's apartment in London; **100** below William Yeoward's house in the country; **101** Dominique Lubar's apartment in London; **102** Jamie Drake's apartment in New York; **103** above Moussie Sayers of Nordic Style's house in London; **103** below Jamie Drake's apartment in New York; **104** above Moussie Sayers of Nordic Style's house in London; **104** below Caroline Clifton-Mogg's house in London; 105 Moussie Sayers of Nordic Style's house in London; **106** above Véronique Lopez's house from Casa Lopez; **106** below Nathalie Hambro's house in London; **107** above & below Nathalie Hambro's apartment in London; **108-109** Kate Dyson of The Dining Room Shop's house in London; **111** Jamie Drake's apartment in New York; **112-113** Anthony Cochrane's apartment in New York; **114** above Josephine Ryan's house in London; **114** below left Caroline Clifton-Mogg's house in London; **114** below right Josephine Ryan's house in London; **115** Josephine Ryan's house in London; **116** Carefree & Figlar; **117** above Lena Proudlock of Denim In Style's house in Gloucestershire; **117** below Moussie Sayers of Nordic Style's house in London; **118-119** Michael Coorengel and Jean-Pierre Calvagrac's apartment in Paris; **120-121** William Yeoward's house in the country; **122-123** Michael Coorengel and Jean-Pierre Calvagrac's apartment in Paris; **124-125** Dining Room designed by Stephanie Stokes Inc., Interior Design; **126-127** Kate Dyson of The Dining Room Shop's house in London; **128-129** Stephane & Victoria du Roure's house in New Hampshire; **130-131** Véronique Lopez's house from Casa Lopez; **132-133** Dominique Lubar's apartment in London; **134-135** Reem Acra's apartment in New York; **136-137** Home of Peri Wolfman and Charles Gold in Bridgehampton; **138-139** Nathalie Hambro's house in London; **141** Caroline Clifton-Mogg's house in London; **142** above left Josephine Ryan's house in London; **142** above right Véronique Lopez's house from Casa Lopez; **142** below Josephine Ryan's house in London; **143** above & below Véronique Lopez's house from Casa Lopez; **144** Lena Proudlock of Denim In Style's house in Gloucestershire; **144-145** Kate Dyson of The Dining Room Shop's house in London; **146** above Michael Coorengel and Jean-Pierre Calvagrac's apartment in Paris; **146** below Carefree & Figlar; **147** above left Michael Coorengel and Jean-Pierre Calvagrac's apartment in Paris; **147** above right Moussie Sayers of Nordic Style's house in London; **147** below William Yeoward's house in the country; **148-149** Josephine Ryan's house in London; **150-151** Glen Senk and Keith Johnson's house in Philadelphia; **152** Caroline Clifton-Mogg's house in London; **153** Kate Dyson of The Dining Room Shop's house in London; 154 Ann Mob's house in London; **155** above Ann Mollo's house in London; **155** below Stephane and Victoria du Roure's house in New Hampshire; **156** above Moussie Sayers of Nordic Style's house in London; **156** below Josephine Ryan's house in London; **157** Home of Peri Wolfman and Charles Gold in Bridgehampton; **158** Anthony Cochrane's apartment in New York; **159** above Glen Senk and Keith Johnson's house in Philadelphia; **159** below left Jackye Lanham's home in Atlanta; **159** below right Stephanie Reeves' home in Atlanta, Georgia; **160** above & below left Glen Senk and Keith Johnson's house in Philadelphia; **160** below right Josephine Ryan's house in London; 161 Glen Senk and Keith Johnson's house in Philadelphia; 162 Carefree & Figlar; **163** above Carefree & Figlar; **163** Tricia Foley's house on Long Island; **164** Lena Proudlock of Denim In Style's house in Gloucestershire; **165** Nathalie Hambro's house in London; **166** above & below Véronique Lopez's house from Casa Lopez; **166-167** Moussie Sayers of Nordic Style's house in London; **170-171** Moussie Sayers of Nordic Style's house in London; **172** above Dominique Lubar's house in London; **172-173** Daniel Rozensztroch's apartment in Paris; **174-175** Home of Peri Wolfman and Charles Gold in Bridgehampton; **175** Glen Senk and Keith Johnson's house in Philadelphia; **176** above Carefree & Figlar; **176** below Tricia Foley's house on Long Island; **177** Carefree & Figlar; **178** Véronique Lopez's house from Casa Lopez; **179** above Tricia Foley's house on Long Island; **179** above Anthony Cochrane's apartment in New York; **180** Tricia Foley's house on Long Island; **181** Home of Peri Wolfman and Charles Gold in Bridgehampton; **182** Véronique Lopez's house from Casa Lopez; **183** above Nathalie Hambro's house in London; **183** below Tricia Foley's house on Long Island.

index

Page numbers in italics refer
to picture captions

acknowledgements

There can be few greater pleasures than writing a book about something in which you are already passionately interested. China and glass has always fascinated me: a visit to the ceramics or the glass department of the Victoria and Albert museum in London is a revelation; within the tall glass cases, your eye is caught by so many different objects – some cheerful, rough and ready, others refined, elegant and delicate – all charming, imaginative and beautiful.

The skill of china and glassmakers, past and present, is breathtaking; the way they mould and decorate their raw materials, an extraordinary art. It was a great pleasure, whilst doing this book, to see so many beautiful pieces of china and glass that are cared for and loved by their owners and I would very much like to thank the latter for allowing us to root about in the back reaches of their precious china cupboards.

I would also like to thank everyone involved in producing the book: Jacqui Small for encouraging me to do it in the first place, Simon Upton for such sympathetic photographs and Nadine Bazar for finding such interesting locations; Kate John and Polly Boyd for arranging the words so skilfully, and Penny Stock for making the whole book look so seductive.